**Jazz Up
Your Japanese
with
Onomatopoeia**

Jazz Up Your Japanese with Onomatopoeia

For All Levels

Hiroko Fukuda

translation and introduction by Tom Gally

KODANSHA INTERNATIONAL
Tokyo • New York • London

Previously published in Kodansha International's Power Japanese series
under the title *Flip, Slither, & Bang: Japanese Sound and Action Words*
(1993). Now with a new introduction and quizzes.

Distributed in the United States by Kodansha America, Inc., and in the
United Kingdom and continental Europe by Kodansha Europe Ltd.

Published by Kodansha International Ltd., 17–14, Otowa 1-chome,
Bunkyo-ku, Tokyo 112–8652, and Kodansha America, Inc.

First edition, 1993
First trade paperback edition, 2003
18 17 16 15 14 13 12 11 10 09 08   12 11 10 9 8 7 6 5 4

www.kodansha-intl.com

Contents

PREFACE

This book is an introduction to onomatopoeia and mimesis in Japanese through real-life conversations and examples. While presenting some of the most common sound and action words, I've added several other features to make the book even more useful.

The language in the book is natural spoken Japanese. Many people who study outside of Japan get a rude awakening when they first visit: they don't understand what anyone is saying. The reason is that the language they've learned from textbooks is stiff and unnatural, often unlike what is heard in everyday life. As a countermeasure of sorts, the conversations and examples given here are all in an informal spoken style, with a balance between women's and men's language. When you read this book, I hope you will feel as though you're having a nice friendly chat in Japanese, the way it would be done if you were talking to an actual person.

The topics show the real Japan. Contrary to popular belief, few Japanese have much to do with geisha, trade negotiations, or Mt. Fuji during their daily lives. The subject matter taken up in this book show what people actually talk about at home, at work, and at play.

Each of the main vocabulary items is marked G, N, or B (Good, Neutral, or Bad, to show if its sense is positive, neutral, or negative). After all, nothing is more embarrassing than to use a word that has the right meaning but the wrong connotation.

Brief notes provide information on cultural background. Every language is an essential part of the culture of the people who speak it, a window on the country's history and ways of thinking. That's why every language is different and difficult and fascinating. Learning another language is worthwhile because it gives you a link to other people, both as a vehicle for sharing ideas and as a practical tool for everyday life. But to master a language, you need more than grammar and vocabulary, so I've scattered notes throughout this book to provide some basic information about Japanese life and customs.

Typical Japanese names are used in the examples. It's hard to remember unfamiliar names in a foreign language. To help you out in this regard, I've made a point of using the ten most common surnames and a variety of common given names.

Illustrations show the settings of each conversation. If you've never visited Japan, these drawings should help you visualize the speakers and their surroundings.

You can read the book in any order. Some people always start on the first page of a book and read straight through to the last. If you prefer to skip around, though, go right ahead. Read the dialogues first or save them for later. Or use the index to look up particular words of interest.

Finally, I would like to express my appreciation to Kodansha International editors Michael Brase and Shigeyoshi Suzuki, who encouraged me to write this unwritable book, and to Tom Gally, who not only translated the book but also wrote the Introduction. I would also like to thank Joe D. Betts and Robert J. Betts for their timely advice.

Hiroko Fukuda

INTRODUCTION An Overview of Onomatopoeia

Onomatopoeia—the use of words whose sounds suggest their meanings—is one of the most enjoyable and fascinating features of the Japanese language. With onomatopoeia, you can express a vast range of meanings in many situations. Onomatopoeia is also, however, one of the hardest parts of the language for English speakers to master, simply because it is so different from English onomatopoeia. Nevertheless, you need to come to grips with it in order to speak and understand Japanese properly.

This first chapter outlines the main features of Japanese onomatopoeia together with the related concepts of sound symbolism and mimesis. Here we will give you the large picture, leaving the details to the situational dialogues in the rest of the book. The big picture can be summarized thus: Japanese onomatopoeia is a well-developed, intricate system, a world unto itself. It is based on imitating natural sounds, but it also mimics, or represents, conditions and states that produce no sound at all. The words making up this system have not been created in a random manner, but follow certain rules and conventions. The vast majority of these words are not general purpose words (like とても *totemo* very) that can be used relatively freely; they are, on the contrary, specific in meaning and restrictive concerning which words they combine with. Further, many of these words have more than one meaning or sense and can be used as more than one part of speech.

With the larger picture as given below in mind, you should find it

much easier to understand, acquire, and reproduce Japanese onomatopoeia. This is no small thing, for onomatopoeia is one of the
most fundamental, characteristic, and lively aspects of the Japanese
language. For native Japanese speakers, onomatopoeia are not just
words; they are windows through which they view the world. These
words represent, to a considerable extent, the Japanese perception
of life.

Before going on to take a closer look at Japanese onomatopoeia,
however, let's first take a look at the relationship between sound and
meaning in general.

Sound and Meaning

In English, Japanese, and all other human languages, the pronuncia-
tions of most words have no relation to what they mean. The English
word *book*, for example, is made up of three sounds—*b, oo,* and *k*—
that have nothing to do with the word's meaning. Other words with
meanings similar to *book*—like *volume* and *edition*—are made up of
different sounds. Words with sounds similar to *book*—like *boot* and
bike and *hook*—have meanings that are completely different. There
is nothing "booklike" about the sounds *b, oo,* and *k*.

The same is true of most Japanese words. Take the words いえ ie,
うち uchi, and すみか sumika, all of which are types of dwelling. None
of them is pronounced in a way that indicates the meaning of the
word. They are simply sounds, or words, that society has accepted as
referring to certain objects.

But both English and Japanese do have exceptions—words whose
sounds do say something about their meanings. One example of this
are words that describe sounds.

Onomatopoeia in English

In English, how would you describe the sound of a pebble dropping into a still pond? *Plop.* What about a soft blow to a person's head? *Bop.* A horse's footstep? *Clop.* Liquid being spilled onto the floor? *Slop.* Someone falling exhausted onto a couch? *Flop.*

These words—*plop, bop, clop, slop,* and *flop*—are similar in both sound and meaning. They all end with -*op,* and they all refer to the sound of one object striking another. That impact sound is also similar to the sound of their final consonant, *p.* When you say a word ending in *p,* your lips come together quickly and then open again with a short burst of air. That impact of your lips against each other is reminiscent of the sound of pebbles plopping in ponds and tired people flopping onto couches.

The words *bash, clash, crash, smash,* and *splash* are similar. They all share the same last sound, and they all refer to the sound of one object striking another, just like the *plop* group. But there's a difference. While the words that end in -*op* refer to short, hollow sounds, the sounds expressed by the -*ash* words are longer and noisier.

You can see the difference in these sentences:

Fred *bopped* his head against the tree limb.

Fred *bashed* his head against the tree limb.

Or, suppose you were standing next to a bucket of water under an apple tree and one of the following happened:

An apple fell into the bucket with a *plop.*

An apple fell into the bucket with a *splash.*

Most likely your chances of getting wet would be higher with *splash* than with *plop.*

Just as the short, percussive final *p* in *bop* and *plop* suggests a short, percussive sound, the longer and noisier *sh* in *bash* and *splash* suggests a longer and noisier sound. There is clearly a relation between the pronunciation of the words and their meanings.

Words like *bop* and *bash* and *plop* and *splash*, in which the pronunciation imitates an actual sound, are called "onomatopoeia." The word "onomatopoeia" came into English through Latin from the original Greek, in which it was coined from the roots *onoma*, meaning "name," and *poiein*, "to make." Thus "onomatopoeia" originally meant the making of names for things; in English, it now refers specifically to the making of words that imitate sounds.

English has hundreds of onomatopoeic words. They include the sounds made by animals:

bow-wow	meow
caw	neigh
chirp	oink
growl	tweet
hiss	twitter

They also include sounds of things moving or being moved:

bang	pop
clatter	rattle
crash	rumble
flutter	snap
jangle	whir

Many onomatopoeic words describe how people talk:

chatter	murmur
grumble	mutter
hiss	purr
jabber	stutter
moan	yackety-yack

Some onomatopoeic words have evolved from strictly referring to sounds to indicating a characteristic, condition, or action that does not necessarily produce a sound.

rattle (sound of colliding objects)	$\longrightarrow$ to rattle (befuddle)
piss (sound of urine)	$\longrightarrow$ to piss off (make angry)
bump (sound of objects colliding)	$\longrightarrow$ to bump into (meet by accident)
clash (loud noise)	$\longrightarrow$ armies clash (come into conflict)
click (brief sound)	$\longrightarrow$ they clicked from the beginning (hit it off)
croak (sound of frog)	$\longrightarrow$ the old codger croaked this morning (die)
crunch (noisy, crackling sound)	$\longrightarrow$ an energy crunch (critical moment)
squawk (screech)	$\longrightarrow$ squawking about the long hours (complain)

As might be guessed from the above, and in great contrast to Japanese, one of the chief characteristics of English onomatopoeia is that the original simple words that imitate a sound in nature are converted to verbs and other parts of speech: e.g., the simple sound "pop" becomes "pop you on the head," "pop the question," "the words popped out of my mouth," or even parts of other words (popcorn, pop quiz).

These examples give us an idea of why onomatopoeia is used at all, whether in Japanese or English. It is for effect, to give one's speech more impact, to get across one's thoughts or feelings more precisely. For instance, it is much more forceful to say, "The car screeched to a halt" than "The car came to a halt with a loud sound." Or "The top of my ice cream cone fell splat (with the noise of something soft hitting a flat surface) on the head of the bald person sitting in front of me." Or "The car zoomed (went rapidly) down the street." As you can see, onomatopoeia makes your language not only more vivid but more precise too.

Sound Symbolism

Sometimes the sounds of words not only correspond to actual acoustic sounds but carry other, less clearly defined meanings as well. In English, for example, many words that begin with *gl-*, such as *glance, glare, gleam, glimpse, glint, glitter,* and *glow,* are related to light or vision. Several words ending in *-dle* refer to wasting time: *dawdle, diddle, fiddle.* Even the vowel sound can suggest a meaning, as in words for smallness like *little, mini,* and *itsy-bitsy,* all of which have a short *i* vowel sound.

This correspondence between pronunciation and a broader range of meanings is called *sound symbolism.* But unlike onomatopoeia, with sound symbolism there is little or no relationship between the speech sounds themselves and actual sounds in the real world. While the sounds in the words *smash* and *growl* may imitate sounds in nature, there is no natural sound that requires that the consonant cluster *st-* should mean "constant, reliable," as it does in *steady, stable, sturdy, stalwart, staunch, steadfast,* and *stout.*

Onomatopoeia and Sound Symbolism in Japanese

As in English, onomatopoeic words in Japanese are meant to imitate the sounds of nature, but whether you think they do this successfully depends on your cultural background. Each culture and language seems to represent natural sounds in a slightly different way. Here are some very simple Japanese onomatopoeic words.

どん don (explosive sound)

ばん ban (bursting sound)

きい kī (screeching sound)

うう ū (groaning sound)

どう dō (sound of a heavy object moving)

だあん dān (sound of a gunshot or explosion)

ぜえぜえ zēzē (wheezing sound)

じいじい jījī (sizzling sound)

Here are words that imitate the sounds of animals.

きいきい kīkī (monkey)

ぐうぐう gūgū (pigeon)

けろけろ kerokero (frog)

こけこっこ kokekokko (rooster)

こんこん konkon (fox)

ひひいん hihīn (horse)

ぶうぶう būbū (pig)

もうもう mōmō (cow)

Just as in English, Japanese has many words that imitate the sound of things moving or being moved.

ずしずし zushizushi (reverberations made by a large object or animal)

ざあざあ zāzā (sound of the movement of a large amount of water, sand, or powdery material)

ごろごろ gorogoro (thunder)

がつん gatsun (a hard angular object hitting another hard object)

だらだら daradara (dropping sounds of a sticky substance)

そよそよ soyosoyo (the blowing of a refreshing breeze)

しゃりしゃり sharishari (the rubbing together of hard, thin objects)

ぎゃあぎゃあ gyāgyā (the noise of excited animals or the cries of human beings)

Of course, among Japanese onomatopoeia there are many words that refer to people talking.

ぺちゃぺちゃ pechapecha (continuous noisy talking)

べちゃべちゃ bechabecha (uncontrolled noisy talking)

くどくど kudokudo (persistently repetitious)

こそこそ kosokoso (clandestine)

のらりくらり norarikurari (pointless wandering)

ずけずけ zukezuke (without holding back)

ひそひそ hisohiso (in whispers)

べらべら berabera (continuously and trivially)

Japanese has many words that appear to be onomatopoeia (i.e., imitate a sound) but actually refer to outward appearance—an action or condition that does not necessarily involve sound.

しいん shīn (silence)

ひんやり hinyari (to feel not unpleasantly cold)

ごちゃごちゃ gochagocha (for things to be intermixed and in no particular order)

じろじろ jirojiro (to stare, ogle)

ぴったり pittari (to match perfectly without gaps or discrepancies)

じわじわ jiwajiwa (for something to undergo slow but steady progress or change)

おどおど odoodo (to be uneasy from worry or fear)

Fortunately for the student, Japanese onomatopoeia are not formed randomly but follow certain rules and conventions. Some of these rules will be touched upon later. Here we would like to say a little about the role that sound symbolism plays in the formation of onomatopoeia.

As pointed out earlier, sound symbolism refers not to words as a whole but to certain parts that make up words—parts that have a significance all their own. In the English language we saw how *gl* referred to light or vision in such words as "glance," "glare," and "gleam." A similar thing can be found in Japanese.

Sound Symbolism in Japanese Vowels

The five Japanese vowels (*a, i, u, e, o*) have symbolic meanings when used in onomatopoeia. The vowel *i* refers to something small or quick, while *a, u,* and *o* are, in contrast, used to refer to something larger and slower. *E* is less often used in onomatopoeia than the other vowels and usually has negative connotations.

Here are some examples of *i* indicating something small or quick.

ちびちび chibichibi (doing something a little at a time)

きらきら kirakira (a small light source blinking repeatedly)

いそいそ isoiso (to move in a lively fashion)

しとしと shitoshito (rain falling quietly in small drops)

Here is an example of *a* indicating a clear sound, *i* a high-pitched sound, and *o* a low-pitched sound.

かんかん kankan (the clear sound made by a small, hard object repeatedly striking the surface of an extremely hard, relatively small object)

きんきん kinkin (a high-pitched, sharp, metallic sound)

こんこん konkon (the low-pitched sound of a small, hard object striking a hard surface)

Examples of *e* with a negative connotation include:

へとへと hetoheto (complete exhaustion)

へらへら herahera (laughing foolishly)

へなへな henahena (breaking or bending easily under pressure)

べろん beron (sticking out one's tongue)

めきめき mekimeki (undergoing remarkable or outstanding change; see page 158) would seem to be an exception to this rule, but in fact the original meaning of the word had a negative nuance, referring to something making a creaking or rasping sound or simply falling apart.

Another characteristic of vowels is that short vowels suggest that a sound is short or that an action covers only a short distance in time or space, while long vowels indicate a long sound or an action that is more prolonged in either time or space. For example, じっと立つ jitto tatsu means "to stand without moving," while じいっと立つ jītto tatsu, which uses the long vowel *ii*, means "to stand without moving for a long time." Similarly, both ぱっと開く patto hiraku and ぱあっと開く pātto hiraku mean "to open, to spread out," but the version with the long vowel *ā* suggests that the motion expands more widely.

Sound Symbolism in Japanese Consonants

As for the consonants, *k* usually indicates a light or high-pitched sound. It is used in contrast to *g*, which is a heavier, duller, or lower-pitched sound.

かあかあ kākā (bird's cry)

があがあ gāgā (duck's call, human wailing, loud mechanical sound)

かん kan (high drawn-out sound of light metal objects striking together)

がん gan (drawn-out sound of metal objects forcefully striking to-ether)

The consonant *s* indicates friction (with a light or small connotation) and is contrasted to *z* (including じ ji), which refers to something dull, heavy, big, or dirty.

さあっと sātto (sound of quick, light movement)

ざあっと zātto (sound of a large amount of liquid, sand, or grainy substance suddenly flowing forth, dropping, or collapsing)

さくさく sakusaku (light, repetitive sound of a sandlike substance being moved, mixed, or pushed)

ざくざく zakuzaku (sound of a hard, rough, grainy substance mixing together)

T (including ち chi) indicates a light sound (with connotations of sharpness, lightness, or smallness) and is contrasted to *d* (including ぢ ji and づ zu), with its connotations of heavy, big, dull, or dirty.

とんとん tonton (a light, repetitive striking sound)

どんどん dondon (a strong, repetitive sound of hard objects striking together)

とろっと torotto (the appearance of a viscous, smooth liquid)

どろっと dorotto (the appearance of a highly dense and viscous liquid)

H (including ふ fu) has a pure, light, quiet, or small connotation and is contrasted to *p* (which has a sharp, light, cute, or bouncy connotation) and *b* (which has a dull, heavy, big, or dirty connotation). *H* is referred to as unvoiced (清音 seion), *p* as partially voiced (半濁音 han-dakuon), and *b* as voiced (濁音 dakuon). The partially voiced category applies only to the *h* series of consonants. The consonants *k*, *s*, and *t* come only in unvoiced and voiced versions; they have no partially voiced forms.

はたはた hatahata (sound of cloth, wings, or similar objects catching the wind)

ぱたぱた patapata (sound of thin, light objects flapping or hitting something, or the appearance of hands and feet moving busily)

ばたばた batabata (sound of cloth or other flat objects flapping in the wind or hitting something, or the repetitious sound of wings or hands and feet moving busily in small motions)

はっと hatto (the outward appearance of tension or surprise when coming across something unexpected)

ぱっと patto (the outward appearance of an expected action, change, event, etc.)

ばっと batto (the outward appearance of something suddenly going forcefully into action)

These are some general rules and conventions that apply to sound symbolism in Japanese, but the student must remember that the subject is much more complicated (there is much more room for study if you wish to do it!). Furthermore, this system is not one that is perfectly integrated, but it is the work of Japanese speakers over generations and encompasses many inconsistencies and exceptional cases.

Word Beginning with ち Chi, Indicating Smallness or Quickness

It is interesting to note that some sound symbols form little families or groups that help in learning new onomatopoeia. For example, it seems that ち chi occurs often in reference to something that is small or quick. Here are a few examples:

ちびちび chibichibi (an action that is done not all at one time but repetitively and a little at a time)

ちまちま chimachima (the fact that something is arranged in a small compact unit)

ちょこっと chokotto (the fact of something being of only a small amount, degree, or time)

ちょこんと chokonto (the fact that something is in a single compact unit)

ちょっぴり choppiri (the fact that something is of a very tiny amount, time, or degree)

ちょぼちょぼ chobochobo (the fact that something is sparsely scattered or of a small amount)

ちりんちりん chirinchirin (the repetitive sound of a small bell)

As you become familiar with a good number of onomatopoeia, you will begin to recognize these groupings, which will make the acquisition of new words much easier.

Onomatopoeia and Mimesis

What we have generally been calling onomatopoeia until now is usually divided into at least two categories by Japanese scholars. The first is 擬音語 (*giongo*, or what we would strictly call onomatopoeia), which refers to the imitation of sound. The second category, 擬態語 (*gitaigo*, or mimesis), uses the same techniques as the first but refers to outward appearance or inner psychology rather than sound.

The first category we have covered above, and the second category we have referred to indirectly. Here we will cover mimesis in a little more detail. Mimesis uses the sound symbolism of onomatopoeia, and other structural techniques as well (to be touched on below), to describe things in a way that is less concrete than onomatopoeia but more concrete than nonmimetic words. In fact, many Japanese words of this type have both onomatopoeic (sound-imitating) and mimetic (nonsound) senses. For example, the word ぐいぐい guigui (chugalug; see page 99) refers both to the sound of drinking something without pausing and to the action of doing the same, without the sound. In this case, the same thing can be found in English, where the word "chugalug" imitates a sound but can also be used for the action itself, even though no sound is actually made.

Here are a few examples of words that have both sound (onomatopoeic) and nonsound (mimetic) senses:

ぐうぐう gūgū

Sound: to snore

Nonsound: to sleep soundly

しくしく shikushiku

Sound: to cry continuously while sniffling

Nonsound: a dull continuous pain

じゃりじゃり jarijari

Sound: the rubbing together of grainlike objects or roughly sewn cloth

Nonsound: the feel of a rough texture

ちゃらちゃら charachara

Sound: the striking together of small pieces of metal or hard wood

Nonsound: to attract attention by flirting or being coquettish

Looking at this list, one might come to the conclusion that nonsound (mimetic) usage is simply an extended or figurative development of onomatopoeia that imitates sound. This does, in fact, seem to be the case. On the other hand, there are also mimetic words that have no corresponding onomatopoeic equivalent. For the sake of simplicity, therefore, in this book "onomatopoeia" generally refers not only to sound-imitating words—the normal meaning of "onomatopoeia" in English—but also to nonsound, mimetic words.

Types of Japanese Onomatopoeia

According to their forms or structure, onomatopoeia can be divided into three types, some of which have been touched upon above. Each of these forms connotes certain meanings. Here we will outline the categories with their meanings and some examples. Sometimes the examples given here refer first to one of the several meanings of a word and then, later, to a different sense of the same word. Don't be confused by the fact that the same word is defined in slightly different ways. It is a different sense of the same word that is being referred to.

Onomatopoeia Type 1: Repetitive Onomatopoeia

The first type is repetitive onomatopoeia, in which there is a repetition of certain sounds or syllables within a word. These words are called 畳語 jōgo. Examples of such words are ぴちぴち pichipichi and ちやほや chiyahoya.

When these words refer to a sound or to an action or movement, they usually refer to something that repeats itself or is consecutive or progressive.

くどくど kudokudo (repeating the same thing over and over in detail)

うつらうつら utsura-utsura (to go back and forth between being awake and half asleep)

When referring to conditions and states of being, repetitive onomatopoeia primarily indicates that a static condition has come into being. For example:

べろべろ berobero (a state of total inebriation)

くたくた kutakuta (a condition of total exhaustion)

Another of the conditions indicated by repetitive words is the plural number.

ごほんごほん gohongohon (coughing more than once)

ちょんちょん chonchon (the two marks, 濁点 dakuten [゛], used in such kana as が ga)

Repetitive onomatopoeia can also indicate that something is being checked or confirmed over a period of time.

じろじろ jirojiro (to direct one's gaze repeatedly at something in an offensive way)

しげしげ shigeshige (to direct one's gaze often and earnestly toward something)

Likewise, repetitive onomatopoeia can indicate that something is being checked or confirmed within the confines of a certain space.

きょろきょろ kyorokyoro (to look around nervously at a rare sight, in search for something lost, etc.)

きょときょと kyotokyoto (to direct one's gaze nervously here and there out of uneasiness, fear, etc.)

Onomatopoeia Type 2: Voiced and Unvoiced Consonants

As mentioned in the section titled "Onomatopoeia and Sound Symbolism in Japanese," Japanese onomatopoeia contrasts unvoiced (清音 seion), partially voiced (半濁音 han-dakuon), and voiced (濁音 dakuon) consonants. Examples of this would be はらはら harahara, ぱらぱら parapara, and ばらばら barabara.

We saw earlier (page 18) that unvoiced onomatopoeia tend to refer to something that is pure, light, quiet, and small, while partially voiced words have a sharp, light, cute, or bouncy connotation, and voiced words tend to be dull, heavy, big, or dirty in meaning.

Onomatopoeia Type 3: Word-ending Sounds

"Word-ending sound" (語尾音 gobion) refers to the sound with which an onomatopoeic word ends, of which there are five types: words ending in a glottal stop, words ending in り ri; words ending in ん n; words ending in a long final vowel; and words ending in *syllable* + small つ tsu + *syllable* + り ri (or ん n). Each of these forms has its own connotations. We will look at each of these five types in regard to their connotations when referring to sound, to movement, and to a condition.

■ Glottal Stop Type

A glottal stop occurs when the vocal cords are closed tightly for an instant and then suddenly released. (The sounds at the beginning and middle of the English negative grunt *uh-uh* are glottal stops.) The glottal stop is indicated by a small つ in Japanese script and usually by two t's in romanization. Words ending with a glottal stop may actually end with the glottal stop or they may be, and often are, followed by the particle と to. The version without と to is more abrupt or sudden and more likely to capture instaneously the moment a condition comes into being, rather than a continuous condition. Here we have listed the words with the と to attached.

When referring to sound, the glottal stop type of onomatopoeia indicates that the sound came to an abrupt end. For example:

ばしっと bashitto (sound made when a dry stick or similar object suddenly breaks or strikes another object)

ぶすっと busutto (sound produced when a sticklike object forcefully pierces a soft, thick substance one time)

When referring to movement, the glottal stop type indicates sudden movement, speed, or forcefulness.

ぱっと patto (indicates that a movement, action, change, etc. is sudden and swift)

じろっと jirotto (refers to looking sternly in a certain direction, one time)

In terms of conditions that have already been established, the glottal stop type captures the moment the condition comes into being.

ふわっと fuwatto (captures the moment that something soft and light swells up or rises)

ぼけっと boketto (indicates that the mind has wandered or a lack of attention)

■ り **Ri Type**

As with the glottal stop type, words ending with り ri also have different connotations depending on whether they refer to sound, movement, or an established condition.

When referring to sound, this type indicates that the sound is well rounded and complete in itself (that is, is not abrupt or elongated).

ぺしゃり peshari (the sound of something under pressure being smashed or collapsing)

かちり kachiri (the small sound of a hard metal object striking another object forcefully one time)

When referring to movement, り ri words indicate that the movement has come to a decided, natural conclusion or that the entire process of the movement is comprehensible as a whole. For example:

ころり korori (indicates the rolling action of a spherical or small object, focusing on the fact that the action has been completed and cannot be reversed)

するり sururi (indicates something rapidly slipping away and coming free, with the focus on the results of the slipping-away action)

When referring to conditions that have already been established, り ri words confirm that they have indeed been established and have come to an end (i.e., are not partial or still ongoing)

ぴたり pitari (indicates that one thing closely adheres to another, focusing on the situation after the action has taken place)

ふんわり funwari (indicates that a light object has floated up, focusing on the situation after the action has taken place)

■ ん N Type

As with the glottal stop type and the り ri type, words ending with ん n also have different connotations depending on whether they refer to sound, movement, or an established condition.

When referring to sound, the ん n type indicates that the sound echoes or reverberates. For example:

こんこん konkon (the sound of a dry, repetitive cough, in which the sound is relatively small with little reverberation)

ごほんごほん gohongohon (the resounding, repetitive sound of a wet cough with greater reverberation)

When referring to movement, the ん n type refers to something that rebounds, spreads out, or is particularly forceful (not to something that is confined, controlled, or weak).

ぱたん patan (indicates that a thin, hard object has collided with something else, one time)

ばたん batan (indicates that a hard, heavy object of considerable size has collided with another object, one time)

When referring to established conditions or states, ん n words emphasize the established condition.

どろん doron (indicates that a thick, highly dense liquid is floating, focusing on the condition of floating)

ぷつん　putsun (indicates that something that was continuous has suddenly been broken, focusing on the void thus created and on the fact that the former condition cannot be returned to)

■ **Long Vowel Type**

In this type, the word ends with a long vowel. When referring to sound, it indicates that the sound being imitated is a prolonged one. For example:

さあ　sā (the sound of a machine with the switch on, idling quietly)

すうすう　sūsū (the sound of air passing continuously through a small opening)

When referring to movement or action, the long vowel type indicates that the process is continuous.

ぱあ　pā (indicates that something spreads out all at once with considerable force)

のうのう　nōnō (indicates that someone is stretched out comfortably and taking a rest)

When referring to a condition or state, the long vowel type emphasizes the nature of the condition or state. For example:

ぴたあ　pitā (an emphatic indication that one thing closely adheres to another; more emphatic than ぴた pita)

ふわあ　fuwā (an emphatic indication that a light, soft object expands one time; more emphatic than ふわ fuwa)

■ *Syllable* + **Small** つ **Tsu (Glottal Stop)** + *Syllable* + り **Ri (or** ん **N) Type**

This, the last onomatopoeia type, lends emphasis when referring to a sound. (See page 24 for the meaning of "glottal stop.") Examples show forms ending in both り ri and ん n.

かっちり katchiri (sound of a small, hard object colliding with another; more emphatic than かちり kachiri)

かっちん katchin (sound of a hard object colliding with another, with the sound being short and high-pitched, with some reverberation; more emphatic than かちん kachin)

When referring to movement or action, this type indicates that the movement has come to a decided, natural conclusion and is complete in itself. Examples show forms ending in both り ri and ん n.

ばったり battari (indicates that a standing object or person has suddenly taken a light fall; more emphatic than ばたり batari).

ばっちゃん batchan (indicates that a large object has plunged into water, creating a large splash; more emphatic than ばちゃん bachan)

When referring to a condition or state, this type emphasizes that the condition has come to a decided, natural conclusion and is complete in itself. Examples show forms ending in both り ri and ん n.

ぴったり pittari (indicates that something in progress suddenly comes to a stop, focusing on the resulting condition; more emphatic than ぴたり pitari)

ごっつん gottsun (indicates that a heavy, hard object has collided one time with another object; more emphatic than ごつん gotsun)

We have now looked at three types of onomatopoeia, along with their variations. Most onomatopoeia do not exhibit all these variations. Here are two word groups with their missing types.

ころ koro (a spherical object rolls one time)

　ころころ korokoro (repetitive type, unvoiced)

　missing (repetitive type, partially voiced)

　ごろごろ gorogoro (repetitive type, voiced)

　ころっと korotto (type ending in a glottal stop)

ころり　korori (type ending in a り ri)

ころん　koron (type ending in ん n)

ころう　[usually written ころー] korō (type ending in a long final vowel)

missing (*syllable* + small つ tsu [glottal stop] + *syllable* + り ri [or ん n] type)

ぺた　peta (something adheres to a flat surface)

missing (unvoiced repetitive)

ぺたぺた　petapeta (repetitive type, partially voiced)

べたべた　betabeta (repetitive type, voiced)

ぺたっと　petatto (type ending in a glottal stop)

ぺたり　petari (type ending in り ri)

ぺたん　petan (type ending in ん n)

ぺたあ　petā (type ending in a long final vowel)

ぺったり　pettari and ぺったん pettan (*syllable* + small つ tsu [glottal stop] + *syllable* + り ri [or ん n] type)

Grammatical Function

The grammatical roles that onomatopoeic words play can be categorized as follows, the first being the most characteristic: 1) as adverbs modifying regular verbs (or kanji compounds combined with する suru), either with the particle と to or without it; 2) directly combined with the all-purpose verb する suru (sometimes with と to) or やる yaru; 3) as adjectivelike words combined with the copula だ da (which is sometimes omitted, making the onomatopoeia appear to be the predicate of the sentence); 4) as nominals followed by the particle の no in adjectival phrases; 5) as adverbial phrases followed by に ni.

Now let us look at each of these categories, giving examples from the dialogues that appear in chapters 2 through 12 of this book (with the translations also roughly following the context provided by the dialogues). Remember that many of these words can appear in various grammatical roles, so the one that appears in the list below is only one of several possibilities. You should familiarize yourself with these combinations before going on to the rest of the book, for it is supremely important that you learn the verbs and other words that combine with onomatopoeia if you are to learn the words correctly. In fact, it is by far the best policy to learn them as a unit. と to without parentheses indicates required usage; within parentheses, optional usage; no indication, not used.

As Adverbs Modifying Regular Verbs

1. がんがん飲む gangan nomu (to drink up)
2. ぺこぺこ（と）あたまをさげる pekopeko (to) atama o sageru (to bow repeatedly; to act servilely)
3. ちびちび（と）飲む chibichibi (to) nomu (to drink a little at a time)
4. ぐうっといく gūtto iku (to down a drink)
5. どんどんいく dondon iku (to pick up the pace)

Combined with する Suru or やる Yaru

1. きりきりする kirikiri suru (to be stressed)
2. どたばたする dotabata suru (to be on the go)
3. じたばたする jitabata suru (to panic)
4. すかっとする sukatto suru (to feel refreshed)
5. ぴりぴりする piripiri suru (to be on edge)

As Adjectivelike Words Combined with the Copula だ Da

1. へとへとだ hetoheto da (to be tired out)

2. からからだ karakara da (to be parched)

3. ぼちぼちだ bochibochi da (to be so-so)

4. きちきちだ kichikichi da (to be tight)

5. ぎりぎりだ girigiri da (to be pushed to the limit)

As Nominals Followed by the Particle の No in Adjectival Phrases

1. ずんぐりむっくりの純日本型 zunguri-mukkuri no jun-Nihon-gata (to be a typical chunkily-built Japanese)

2. ぶよぶよのお腹 buyobuyo no onaka (flabby stomach)

3. すべすべのお肌 subesube no ohada (smooth skin)

4. はらはらどきどきの連続 harahara dokidoki no renzoku (a series of suspense-filled moments)

As Adverbial Phrases Followed by に Ni

1. べろべろになる berobero ni naru (to get thoroughly drunk)

2. つるつるになる tsurutsuru ni naru (to become smooth)

3. つやつやになる tsuyatsuya ni naru (to become glistening)

4. ぺちゃんこになる pechanko ni naru (to become flat)

5. ぼさぼさになる bosabosa ni naru (to become unruly, tussled)

An Essential Part of Japanese

Onomatopoeia are more common in speech and informal writing than in official or academic prose, and many of the first words that children learn are onomatopoeia. But that does not mean that onomatopoeia are in general slangy or childish. While in English reduplicated words like *higgledy-piggledy* and *topsy-turvy* have a playful sound, Japanese words with similar repeated forms, like うかうか ukauka and じたばた jitabata, are completely standard and are not childish (except, perhaps, when used by children). While onomatopoeia do appear in serious Japanese journalism and literature—contexts where words like *clickety-clack* and *gibber-jabber* rarely appear in English—they are most frequently found in casual conversation among friends, such as that represented by the dialogues in this book.

Many concepts cannot be expressed clearly in Japanese without the use of onomatopoeia. One reason for this is that, while English often concentrates the meaning in verbs, in Japanese more of the meaning is conveyed by nouns, adjectives, and adverbs. Consider, for example, the many verbs used in English to describe laughter, such as *giggle, snicker, guffaw, titter, snort, chuckle,* and *roar*. Each of these words has a distinct meaning. *Chuckle* describes the laughter of someone who is pleased or happy, while *snicker* suggests that the person is being snide. We can say that someone *chuckled with delight,* but the phrase *snickered with delight* is much less common. The snideness of *snicker* in turn makes the phrase *snickered sarcastically* much more natural than *chuckled sarcastically.*

The words' meanings also depend on the sound of the actual laughter that they describe. *Titter* suggests a high pitch, while *guffaw* is pitched low. Small children *giggle* but rarely *guffaw,* and old men *snort* but usually don't *titter.*

In Japanese, such nuances of meaning are conveyed differently. Everyday Japanese seems to use fewer verbs than English, and the verbs themselves often express less specific meanings than English verbs do. The verb 笑う warau, for example, means not only *laugh* but also *smile* and *make fun of.* Japanese speakers express finer shades of meaning, like the differences among *giggle* and *chuckle* and *guffaw* in English, by choosing from among the language's rich supply of onomatopoeia.

If you have access to a computer that can handle Japanese, try this experiment: Use a Japanese-capable search engine to search the Internet for the phrase と笑った to waratta "laughed." Since と to often connects adverbs to verbs, you will find many examples—mostly from online fiction, but also from other types of writing—of adverbs that are used to modify the verb 笑う warau "laugh." For example:

からからと笑った karakara to waratta (laughed with delight)

くすくすと笑った kusukusu to waratta (let out a suppressed laugh)

けらけらと笑った kerakera to waratta (cackled)

You can try this same experiment with other phrases, like と泣いた to naita "wept" or と落ちた to ochita "fell."

Written Forms

The onomatopoeia covered in this book are all native Japanese words, not borrowings from other languages. Japanese does have many Chinese-based literary words that are similar in form and function to the onomatopoeia discussed here, such as 蕭蕭 shōshō "chilly, melancholy" or 燦燦 sansan "bright, sparkling," but they are rare in speech. And despite the many words taken into Japanese from Western languages, especially English, few if any of those borrowings are used as onomatopoeia.

Onomatopoeia are therefore normally written in kana, not kanji. While most dictionaries and textbooks (including this one) give the words only in hiragana, in other publications the katakana forms are nearly as common. The online archive for one Japanese newspaper, for example, shows 32 examples of the phrase *niyari to waratta* in articles over a period of eight years; 22 of those examples were written in hiragana (にやりと笑った) while the other 10 used katakana (ニヤリと笑った). In many cases, katakana is chosen because it adds emphasis to the word, as italics do in English.

When you come across onomatopoeia in katakana and want to look them up in a dictionary, remember that they may be spelled differently in hiragana. For example, you may see gyūgyū (page 205) written as ギューギュー, but dictionaries and textbooks usually indicate the *ū* sound not with the symbol ー but with the vowel う and spell the word as ぎゅうぎゅう, not ギューギュー, ギュウギュウ, or ぎゅーぎゅー. If you are doing an online search for an onomatopoeic word, you should try several different spellings to cover all the different ways the word may be written.

In Japanese publications, the representation of onomatopoeia is not necessarily consistent within one work, partly for rhetorical reasons and partly because one way simply seems more natural or suitable to a particular writer. This aspect of the language is very much up to the individual. The same also applies to how long vowels are written, whether as kana or as a long dash. In this Introduction we have consistently used hiragana to maintain uniformity.

Making Up New Words

Because of the connection between sound and meaning, new words can be coined with sounds that will suggest what they mean. One particularly productive area for the creation of new words in both English and Japanese is comics. English-language comics are full of sound-effect words like *cha-chunk* to indicate the sound of a rifle being cocked or *thamm* for the sound of a door shutting quickly. Although the readers may have never seen these words before, they understand their meaning not only from the context in which they are used but also from the similarity between their sounds and the sounds of more well-established words. *Cha-chunk,* for example, includes the sounds of *chomp* and *chug* and *plunk* and *bonk,* while *thamm* recalls words like *thump* and *bam.*

Japanese manga are full of similar sound effects. While many of the words that appear within the pictures are listed in dictionaries, others are less well established. In one manga, for example, a blinding flash of light is accompanied by the word キラーン *kirān*. No Japanese dictionary includes this word, but its meaning is clear because of its similarity to words like きらきら kirakira "glittering, sparkling" and きらり kirari "shining briefly." The long *ā* in キラーン kirān adds to the meaning by suggesting that the flash of light lasts for a while or that it remains in the eyes of the people who see it.

The coining of new imitative words is not confined to comics. Many Japanese enliven their informal conversations with sound effects and other expressive words that they coin on the spot using the sounds that are familiar from more well-established words. Their listeners, familiar with those sounds and their associated meanings, immediately grasp what the speaker is trying to say and often smile at the speaker's cleverness in coining the word. Naturally, for learners of the language, the coining of onomatopoeia is something that lies far in the future, only to be attempted after becoming thoroughly familiar with the traditional rules and conventions governing Japanese onomatopoeia. However, a lack of skill in this area should not prevent us from enjoying, to the extent that we can, the innovations that appear in manga and anime.

■ ■ ■

Many students of Japanese regard the most challenging part of the language to be kanji, and some learners believe that by mastering kanji they can master Japanese. While this is certainly true in its own way, there exists essential native Japanese vocabulary that does not rely on kanji. Among this type of vocabulary, an especially important and dynamic role is played by the words that are the subject of this book: onomatopoeia.

A New Lease on Life

Tetsu Takahashi of the Marketing Department at Heiwa Securities and his boss, Section Chief Hideo Satō, drop by a bar after work. The beer has just arrived.

高橋　「きょうは参りました*ね、課長。もう**へとへと**ですよ。」

佐藤　「**がんがん**飲もう。俺がおごるよ。」

高橋　「はあ。ありがとうございます。まあどうぞ。」

（課長のグラスにビールを注ぐ†。ビールがあふれそうになって。）

佐藤　「おうっとっと。…**きりきり**することばっかりで、喉も**からから**だな。」

高橋　「全くですね。一日中**どたばた**して、**ぺこぺこ**頭をさげまわって。」

（佐藤さんにビールを注ぎながら）

佐藤　「ま、こういうときには、**じたばた**したって駄目なもんだよ。」

高橋　「はあ、どうも。（注がれたビールを一口飲んで）…うまい。冷えてる。やっぱり**すかっと**しますね、ビールは。」

佐藤　「**ちびちび**飲んでないで、**ぐうっと**いこうよ、**ぐうっと**。」

（さらに高橋さんにビールを注ぐと、高橋さんは勢いよく飲み干して❖）

高橋　「課長こそ**どんどん**いきましょう。」

（佐藤課長、このところ目立ってきたおなかをさすりながら）

佐藤　「**どんどん**はいいけど、水を飲んでも太る体質✿でね。まあいいか、きょうのところは。」

（課長にビールを注ぎ終えたところに、注文したおつまみがくる。）

店員　「へい、お待ちどう、焼き鳥5人前。」

❀ *Mairu*: to be beaten, defeated, frustrated.
† *Tsugu*: to pour.
❖ *Nomihosu*: to drink to the last drop.
✿ *Taishitsu*: constitution, physical type.

Takahashi:	*Kyō wa mairimashita ne, kachō. Mō hetoheto desu yo.*
Satō:	*Gangan nomō. Ore ga ogoru yo.*
Takahashi:	*Hā. Arigatō gozaimasu. Mā dōzo.* *(Kachō no gurasu ni bīru o tsugu. Bīru ga afuresō ni natte.)*
Satō:	*Ōttotto.... Kirikiri suru koto bakkari de, nodo mo karakara da na.*
Takahashi:	*Mattaku desu ne. Ichinichi-jū dotabata shite, pekopeko atama o sagemawatte.* *(Satō-san ni bīru o tsuginagara)*
Satō:	*Ma, kō iu toki ni wa, jitabata shita tte dame na mon da yo.*
Takahashi:	*Hā, dōmo. (Tsugareta bīru o hitokuchi nonde) ...Umai. Hiete 'ru. Yappari sukatto shimasu ne, bīru wa.*
Satō:	*Chibichibi nonde 'nai de, gūtto ikō yo, gūtto.* *(Sara ni Takahashi-san ni bīru o tsugu to, Takahashi-san wa ikioi yoku nomihoshite)*
Takahashi:	*Kachō koso dondon ikimashō.* *(Satō-kachō, konogoro medatte kita onaka o sasurinagara)*
Satō:	*Dondon wa ii kedo, mizu o nonde mo futoru taishitsu de ne. Mā ii ka, kyō no tokoro wa.* *(Kachō ni bīru o tsugioeta tokoro ni, chūmon shita otsumami ga kuru.)*
Ten'in:	*Hei, omachi-dō, yakitori gonin-mae.*

✳ ✳ ✳

Takahashi:	Today was a real killer, wasn't it, boss. I'm dead tired.
Satō:	What do you say we knock back a few. It's on me.
Takahashi:	Hey, thanks a lot. Here you go. (He pours beer into Satō's glass, almost to overflowing.)
Satō:	Whoa, watch it there.... It's been one thing after another, and my throat's gone bone-dry.

Takahashi: The same here. I've been on the go all day long, out talking up clients.

Satō: (pouring for Takahashi) Well, this is not the time or place to be twiddling our thumbs.

Takahashi: Okay, thanks. (He takes a drink.) Aah, that's nice and cold. Beer sure hits the spot.

Satō: Don't just sip at it! Down the hatch! (Satō fills Takahashi's glass again, and he empties it enthusiastically.)

Takahashi: Come on. You, too, boss. Drink up.

Satō: (rubbing his belly, which has become more noticeable recently) I like my drink as much as the next man, but I put on weight just from drinking water. Oh, well, only for tonight.
(Just as Takahashi finishes pouring some more beer for Satō, the food they ordered arrives.)

Waiter: Here you are. Yakitori for five.

➡ Employees of Japanese companies and other organizations rarely address each other by their given names. They generally use surnames followed by a title (社長 *shachō*, 部長 *buchō*, 課長 *kachō*, 係長 *kakarichō*, etc.). When there's no possibility of confusion, the family name can be dropped.

When drinking socially, people usually pour drinks for one another. In this dialogue, Takahashi pours the first round because he is the lower ranking of the two. For later rounds, either one might pour for the other.

へとへと (hetoheto) N / B
To be completely tired, worn out, exhausted.

❑ 2時間もラッシュの電車に乗って通勤すると、会社に着く頃にはもうへとへとですよ。

Ni-jikan mo rasshu no densha ni notte tsūkin suru to, kaisha ni tsuku koro wa mō hetoheto desu yo.

After a two-hour train commute during the morning rush, I'm dead
on my feet by the time I reach the office.

❏ やっぱり運動不足なんだね。子供の運動会でちょっと走っ
  たらへとへとになったよ。

*Yappari undō-busoku nan da ne. Kodomo no undō-kai de chotto
hashittara hetoheto ni natta yo.*

Sure enough, I'm not getting the exercise I should. Just running a
little at my kid's sports festival completely wiped me out.

がんがん (gangan) N / B

This word describes an extremely strong or violent action.

❏ 席を移ってもいいかしら、冷房ががんがんきいていて落ち
  着かないんですもの。

*Seki o utsutte mo ii kashira, reibō ga gangan kiite ite ochitsukanai n'
desu mono.*

Would you mind if I changed seats? With the air conditioning going
full blast, I'm beginning to feel absolutely uncomfortable.

❏ 浮気がばれて女房にがんがんしぼられまして*ね、当分頭が
  上がりません。

*Uwaki ga barete nyōbō ni gangan shiboraremashite ne, tōbun atama
ga agarimasen.*

When my wife found out I was running around with someone else,
she lowered the boom. Now she's got me under her thumb.

❋ *Shiboru*: to wring, tighten the screws on.

きりきり (kirikiri) N / B

The original meaning of this word is the creaking or scraping sound caused by something being rotated, wrapped, or tightened. It can also describe the motion itself. By extension, *kirikiri* sometimes means "very busy," including the notion of stress or tension caused by haste or impatience (N/B). Another meaning is a sharp, continuous pain, as though a pointed object were being forced into one's body (B).

❏ 忙しいからときりきりしたところで、結果はそう変わらないんですけどね。

Isogashii kara to kirikiri shita tokoro de, kekka wa sō kawaranai n' desu kedo ne.

Just because you're busy and work yourself into a frenzy (work your fingers to the bone), the results aren't all that different, it seems.

❏ 部長の雷が落ちる*たびに、胃がきりきり痛むんです。

Buchō no kaminari ga ochiru tabi ni, i ga kirikiri itamu n' desu.

Every time the division manager goes on one of his rampages, my stomach gets all tied up in knots (starts acting up).

❊ *Kaminari ga ochiru*: to thunder, scold.

からから (karakara) N / B

Completely dry, containing no moisture.

❏ 独身はわびしいですよ。出張から帰ってくると、観葉植物*までからからに枯れているんだから。

Dokushin wa wabishii desu yo. Shutchō kara kaette kuru to, kan'yō-shokubutsu made karakara ni karete iru n' da kara.

Being single is really pathetic. Whenever I come home from a business trip, even my plants are all withered.

❊ *Kan'yō-shokubutsu*: potted (ornamental) plants.

❑ 東京の冬は風邪がはやっても無理ないですね。空気がから
からで喉をいためるんですよ。

*Tōkyō no fuyu wa kaze ga hayatte mo muri nai desu ne. Kūki ga
karakara de nodo o itameru n' desu yo.*

It's no wonder so many people in Tokyo get colds during the winter.
The air's bone-dry and wreaks havoc on your throat.

どたばた (dotabata) B

This word describes the sound or action of flying, jumping, or running around. By extension, it also means to rush wildly from place
to place without being able to settle down. The word sometimes
suggests a criticism of the person performing such an action or of
the action itself. When used by the speaker about himself or his
associates, it includes a sense of humility and embarrassment.

❑ うちでは子供がどたばたしているもので、落ち着いて本も
読めないんですよ。

*Uchi de wa kodomo ga dotabata shite iru mono de, ochitsuite hon mo
yomenai n' desu yo.*

With the children rampaging around the house, I can't get enough
peace and quiet to even read a book.

❑ きょうは社内の引っ越しで一日中どたばたしてしまいまして
ね、仕事にならなかったんですよ。

*Kyō wa shanai no hikkoshi de ichinichi-jū dotabata shite shimaimashite
ne, shigoto ni naranakatta n' desu yo.*

Today was moving day at the office, so everyone was running around
like chickens with their heads cut off. Nobody got a bit of work
done.

ぺこぺこ (pekopeko) B

To bow one's head repeatedly in a fawning or groveling manner.

❏ 営業をやっている悲しさで、つい誰にでもぺこぺこしてしまうんですよ。

Eigyō o yatte iru kanashisa de, tsui dare ni de mo pekopeko shite shimau n' desu yo.

The sad part of being in sales is that you end up bowing and scraping to anything that moves.

❏ あなた、ぺこぺこ謝ってばかりいないで、何とか言ったらどうなの。

Anata, pekopeko ayamatte bakari inai de, nan to ka ittara dō na no.

Listen, honey. Don't just stand there apologizing like a fool. Explain yourself.

➥ As a sign of respect, bowing (お辞儀 *ojigi*) is deeply ingrained in Japanese life. People bow to greet others, to say good-bye, to show respect, to make a request, and to apologize. With so many uses, it's natural that there should be many types of bows. The three main categories, depending on the angle of the bow, are 会釈 *eshaku*, a slight bow, a nod of the head; 敬礼 *keirei*, a full bow, a respectful bow; and 最敬礼 *saikeirei*, a very low bow, a worshipful bow. The deeper the bow, the greater the respect.

When standing up, you can do an *eshaku* just by tipping your head forward slightly. This casual bow is appropriate, for example, when greeting an acquaintance on the street. For the more formal *keirei*, stand with heels together and toes slightly spread, look at the ground about a yard in front of you, and bow from the waist. Men usually keep their arms straight down at their sides, while women let their arms swing forward naturally as they bow. The deepest, most respectful bow, *saikeirei*, is performed from a motionless standing position, with the body bent sharply at the waist and the arms held straight down toward the knees. This bow was originally reserved for gods or emperors, though now you may see it employed on other formal occasions as well.

If seated on the floor, take the 正座 *seiza* position (legs folded under, knees together, bottom resting on your feet, back straight, and, ideally, one of your big toes resting on the other), place your hands on the floor in front of you, and bow from the waist with your face pointed toward your hands. For the *eshaku*, bend your body forward about 15°C; for the *keirei*, about 45°C; and for the *saikeirei*, until your nose is nearly touching your hands.

The most common mistake non-Japanese make when bowing is to bend from the neck. While you may amuse your friends with your imitation of a goose, you're better off, for all but the most casual *eshaku*, if you bend from the waist. Another mistake, made by Japanese as well, is to bow more than necessary. Repeated bowing is appropriate when apologizing or making requests, but overly enthusiastic bowing—and this is the nuance of *pekopeko*—gives the impression of being unnecessarily servile.

じたばた (jitabata) B

To flail one's arms and legs around. By extension, to panic or become flustered when trying to confront some imminent problem.

❏ うちの子、歯医者さんが嫌いでね、手足をじたばたさせて抵抗するから困るわ。

Uchi no ko, haisha-san ga kirai de ne, te-ashi o jitabata sasete teikō suru kara komaru wa.

Our kid really hates the dentist. He wriggles like the dickens and simply refuses to cooperate.

❏ 何をやってもうまくいかないときには、じたばたしない方が賢明ですよ。

Nani o yatte mo umaku ikanai toki ni wa, jitabata shinai hō ga kenmei desu yo.

When things don't work out no matter what, you're better off just staying cool and collected.

すかっと (sukatto) G

Clear, refreshing. Free from bad feelings.

❏ 山に登ってすかっとした青空を見ていると、気持ちまですかっとしますよ。

Yama ni nobotte sukatto shita aozora o mite iru to, kimochi made sukatto shimasu yo.

When you climb to the top of a mountain and look up into a clear, blue sky, you can't help feeling like a new man (like a million bucks).

❏ 友達と長電話して愚痴*を聞いてもらったら、すかっとしたわ。

Tomodachi to naga-denwa shite guchi o kiite morattara, sukatto shita wa.

I had a long talk with a friend over the phone and got a lot out of my system. Now I really feel great (on top of the world).

❀ *Guchi*: complaints, grievances.

❏ 夕べ飲み過ぎましてね、けさからどうもすかっとしないんです。

Yūbe nomisugimashite ne, kesa kara dōmo sukatto shinai n' desu.

I drank too much last night and just don't feel myself today.

ちびちび (chibichibi) N / B

To do something slowly and steadily, not all at once. Sometimes used to suggest stinginess.

❏ 日本酒は寿司屋で寿司を握ってもらいながらちびちび飲むのが最高ですよ。

*Nihon-shu wa sushi-ya de sushi o nigitte morainagara chibichibi nomu
no ga saikō desu yo.*

There's nothing like sipping away at your sake in a sushi shop while
they're making the sushi for you.

□ 僕はちびちび倹約するというのが苦手で、いつも女房にしか
られているんです。

*Boku wa chibichibi ken'yaku suru to iu no ga nigate de, itsumo nyōbō
ni shikararete iru n' desu.*

My wife always bawls me out because I'm no good at pinching pen-
nies.

ぐうっと／ぐっと (gūtto/gutto) G / N

The basic meaning of these two words is to concentrate all one's
energy to perform an action (N). They can also be used to express a
big change or difference from a preceding condition or a strong emotion (N) or a feeling that seems to take one's breath away (G/N).
Gūtto and *gutto* can be considered synonymous, but the former expresses a stronger or more prolonged action, change, or emotion.

□ 彼の言動*には頭にくるでしょうが、そこはぐっとこらえてくだ
さい。

*Kare no gendō ni wa atama ni kuru deshō ga, soko wa gutto koraete
kudasai.*

His behavior probably pisses you off, but try not to let it get you
down.

❀ *Gendō*: speech and action.

❏ 美恵子ちゃん、大学に入ったら、ぐうっと大人びちゃって*見違えたよ。

Mieko-chan, daigaku ni haittara, gūtto otonabichatte michigaeta yo.

Since Mieko started college, she's suddenly starting acting so adult she seems like a different person (you wouldn't recognize her).

❀ *Otonabiru*: to look and act grown-up.

❏ 目に涙をためて彼女に謝られたときには、ぐうっときちゃったね。

Me ni namida o tamete kanojo ni ayamarareta toki ni wa, gūtto kichatta ne.

She had tears in her eyes when she said she was sorry. It really got to me.

どんどん (dondon) N

This word describes an action that proceeds continuously and vigorously from one step to the next, without delay or hesitation.

❏ サラリーマンはつまりません*よ、働けば働いただけどんどん儲かるというのならいいんですがね。

Sararīman wa tsumarimasen yo, hatarakeba hataraita dake dondon mōkaru to iu no nara ii n' desu ga ne.

It's a drag being a salaryman. I only wish the money would come in as fast as I'm scrambling to make it.

❀ *Tsumarimasen (tsumaranai)*: boring, tedious.

❏ お父さんと買い物にいくのはいやだわ。だってひとりでどんどん勝手に行っちゃうんだもの。

Otōsan to kaimono ni iku no wa iya da wa. Datte hitori de dondon katte ni itchau n' da mono.

I hate going shopping with my dad. He just barges on ahead all by himself.

A New Lease on Life

Fill in the blanks with one of the words studied in this chapter: へ とへと hetoheto, がんがん gangan, きりきり kirikiri, からから karakara, どたばた dotabata, ぺこぺこ pekopeko, じたばた jitabata, す かっと sukatto, ちびちび chibichibi, ぐうっと／ぐっと gūtto/gutto, どん どん dondon. There are at least two sentences for each word. Answers are on page 217.

1 そう（　　　　）怒らなくたっていいじゃないか。

Sō (　　　　) okoranakuta tte ii ja nai ka.

You don't have to get so hot under the collar.

2 何かあったのかなあ。課長ったら、朝から（　　　　）してい るね。

Nani ka atta no ka nā. Kachō ttara, asa kara (　　　　) shite iru ne.

I wonder what's up. The boss has been running around in a frenzy since morning.

3 きょうは朝から晩まで歩き回って（　　　　）になっちゃったよ。

Kyō wa asa kara ban made arukimawatte (　　　　) ni natchatta yo.

I've been walking around all day (from dawn to dusk), and I'm dead tired.

4 昨日ウイスキーを飲みすぎたのか、夜中に胃が（　　　　）痛 くなった。

Kinō uisukī o nomisugita no ka, yonaka ni i ga (　　　　) itaku natta.

Maybe I drank a little too much whiskey yesterday. In the middle of the night I suddenly got these shooting stomach pains.

5 朝から怒鳴りすぎて、喉が（　　　　）だ。

Asa kara donarisugite, nodo ga (　　　　) da.

Too much shouting from morning on has made my throat as dry as a bone.

6 洗濯物が（　　　　）に乾いているわ。

Sentakumono ga (　　　　) ni kawaite iru wa.

The laundry is completely dry.

7 夕べは隣の家のステレオが（　　　　）鳴っていて、うるさくて眠れなかったわ。

Yūbe wa tonari no ie no sutereo ga (　　　　) natte ite, urusakute nemurenakatta wa.

The stereo next-door was blasting away last night, and I couldn't get any sleep.

8 何をやってもうまくいかなくて、もう（　　　　）だよ。

Nani o yatte mo umaku ikanakute, mō (　　　　) da yo.

Nothing seems to go right, no matter what. I'm absolutely done in.

9 何を（　　　　）しているの？ちょっと静かにしてよ。

Nani o (　　　　) shite iru no? Chotto shizuka ni shite yo.

What's the hubbub all about? Keep the noise down a bit.

10 会社が倒産して（　　　　）頭を下げまわったのはつらかったな。

Kaisha ga tōsan shite (　　　　) atama o sagemawatta no wa tsurakatta na.

After the company went bankrupt, it wasn't much fun going around to apologize to one and all for the fiasco.

11 下の人には威張るくせに、上の人には（ 　　　　 ）する人って嫌だね。

Shita no hito ni wa ibaru kuse ni, ue no hito ni wa (　　　) suru hito tte iya da ne.

I hate people who are high-handed with those below but fawn over those above.

12 喜劇はいいけど、（ 　　　　 ）しているだけじゃ面白くないね。

Kigeki wa ii kedo, (　　　) shite iru dake ja omoshiroku nai ne.

Comedies are fine, but they're not that interesting if they're just a lot of slapstick.

13 試験の前の日に（ 　　　 ）したって遅いよ。

Shiken no mae no hi ni (　　　) shita tte osoi yo.

It's a little late to suddenly get all busy the day before the test.

14 天気がいいと、気持ちまで（ 　　　 ）するね。

Tenki ga ii to, kimochi made (　　　) suru ne.

When the weather's good, it makes you feel great inside.

15 （ 　　　　 ）した顔して、何かいいことでもあったの？

(　　　) shita kao shite, nani ka ii koto de mo atta no?

Judging by the look on your face, you don't seem to have a worry in the world. Did something good happen?

16 苦しいときほど、（ 　　　 ）しないほうがいいもんだよ。

Kurushii toki hodo, (　　　) shinai hō ga ii mon da yo.

The tougher things get, the better it is for you to keep cool and not strike out blindly.

17 （ 　　　　 ）小銭をためておいたら、結構な額になっていたんだ。

(　　　　) *kozeni o tamete oitara, kekkō na gaku ni natte ita n' da.*

When I saved up small change a little at a time, it came to quite a
　　good sum.

18 このお酒はなかなか手に入らないから（　　　　）飲んでい
るんだ。

Kono osake wa nakanaka te ni hairanai kara (　　　　) *nonde iru n' da.*

This sake is hard to come by, so I'm drinking it a little at a time.

19 たくさん作ったから、遠慮なく（　　　　）食べてね。

Takusan tsukutta kara, enryonaku (　　　　) *tabete ne.*

I made a lot, so eat your fill and don't hold back.

20 しばらく会わないうちに（　　　　）背が伸びたね。

Shibaraku awanai uchi ni (　　　　) *se ga nobita ne.*

Since I saw her last a while back, she has really shot up.

21 （　　　　）授業が進むから、ついていけないんだ。

(　　　　) *jugyō ga susumu kara, tsuite ikenai n' da.*

The class just keeps moving ahead faster and faster, and I can't keep
　　up.

22 思わず涙が出そうになったけど、（　　　　）こらえた。

Omowazu namida ga desō ni natta kedo, (　　　　) *koraeta.*

I was suddenly on the verge of tears, but somehow I managed to
　　hold them back.

A Business Lunch

Ken'ichi Yamamoto of the Tokyo trading house Meiji Shōkai is discussing business over lunch with Tadashi Horiuchi of the trading house Shōwa Shōji, which is headquartered in Osaka.

堀内　「もうかりまっか。」

山本　「まあまあですね。でも下半期はがくんと落ち込むんじゃ
　　　ないですか。営業はぴりぴりしてますよ。おたく＊はどう
　　　ですか。」

堀内　「やあ、ぼちぼちでんな。うちとこもうかうかしてられまへ
　　　んわ。」

山本　「どこでも同じですね。ところで例の†件ですが、予算が
　　　きちきちで……。この間の額で何とかなりませんか。お支
　　　払いはきちんとしますから。」

堀内　「そうですかあ。いやあ、難儀ですなあ。うちもぎりぎり
　　　でんねん。」

山本　「そこのところを何とかのんで＊いただけないでしょうか。
　　　この通りです。✿」（と山本さんが頭を下げる）

堀内　「つろおますなあ、山本さんにそない言われたら。そや
　　　けどすんなりはいどうぞ、言うわけにもいきまへんやろ。
　　　こっちのつらい立場もわかってほしおますなあ。」

山本　「それはごもっとも＊です。しかし、堀内さん、困りました
　　　ねえ……。」

堀内　「ほな、よろしおます。これ以上ずるずる延ばすわけにも
　　　いきまへんやろし、勉強さしてもろて、端数をすっぱり切
　　　り捨てるいうことでどないでっしゃろ。」

山本　「そこまでおっしゃるのなら、ずばりその線で＊手を打ち
　　　ましょう。よろしくお願いします。そうと決まったら、どう
　　　です。ひとつビールでも。」

堀内　「おおきに。あんじょうたのんまっさ。」

❀ *Otaku*: somewhat respectful term for someone of approximately the same status but with whom one is not on the most intimate terms: "you, your family, your place of business."

† *Rei no*: (the matter) in question.

❖ *Nomu*: agree to, accept.

✿ *Kono tōri desu*: "(I am) in this manner"; said when bowing and asking a favor.

✢ *(Go)mottomo*: natural, understandable, justifiable.

♣ *Sono sen de*: along those lines.

Horiuchi:	*Mōkarimakka.*
Yamamoto:	*Māmā desu ne. Demo shimohan-ki wa gakunto ochikomu n' ja nai desu ka. Eigyō wa piripiri shite 'masu yo. Otaku wa dō desu ka.*
Horiuchi:	*Yā, bochibochi den na. Uchi toko mo ukauka shite 'raremahen wa.*
Yamamoto:	*Doko de mo onaji desu ne. Tokoro de rei no ken desu ga, yosan ga kichikichi de.... Kono aida no gaku de nan to ka narimasen ka. Oshiharai wa kichinto shimasu kara.*
Horiuchi:	*Sō desu kā. Iyā, nangi desu nā. Uchi mo girigiri den nen.*
Yamamoto:	*Soko no tokoro o nan to ka nonde itadakenai deshō ka. Kono tōri desu. (to Yamamoto-san ga atama o sageru)*
Horiuchi:	*Tsurō 'masu nā, Yamamoto-san ni sonai iwaretara. Soyakedo sunnari hai dōzo, iu wake ni mo ikimahen yaro. Kotchi no tsurai tachiba mo wakatte hoshi omasu nā.*
Yamamoto:	*Sore wa gomottomo desu. Shikashi, Horiuchi-san, Komarimashita nē.*
Horiuchi:	*Hona, yoroshi omasu. Kore ijō zuruzuru nobasu wake ni mo ikimahen yaro shi, benkyō sashite morote, hasū o suppari kirisuteru iu koto de donai dessharo.*

Yamamoto: *Soko made ossharu no nara, zubari sono sen de te o uchi-mashō. Yoroshiku onegai shimasu. Sō to kimattara, dō desu. Hitotsu bīru de mo.*

Horiuchi: *Ōki ni. Anjō tanonmassa.*

* * *

Horiuchi: How's business?

Yamamoto: Pretty good. But it looks as though we're in for a tumble in the second half (of the fiscal year). Our sales people are starting to get jittery. How are things at your place?

Horiuchi: We're managing somehow, but we'll have to keep on our toes, too.

Yamamoto: It's the same all over. Now, about that deal, our budget is tight as a drum.... And the price you mentioned, do you think you could do something about that? We'll pay promptly, right on the dot.

Horiuchi: Well, well, well. That places me in a difficult position. Our profit margin would be cut to the bone.

Yamamoto: Can't you find some way to work around that? As a favor to me. (Yamamoto bows his head.)

Horiuchi: That really puts me on the spot, expressing it like that. You know, I can't say, "Sure, fine with me," just like that. You need to understand how tough our situation is here.

Yamamoto: I get your point, but now that really pushes me up against the wall.

Horiuchi: All right, then. We can't let this drag on forever. I'll offer you a discount. Suppose we just round off the price?

Yamamoto: If you're willing to go with that, it's settled. Now that that's out of the way (concluded), how about a beer?

Horiuchi: Thanks. It's a deal.

➡ If Horiuchi's conversation seems strange to you, that's because he's speaking the Osaka dialect of Japanese. His first question, もうかりまっか (もうかりますか in standard Japanese), is a customary greeting in Osaka, meaning "Have you been making a lot of money?" To a Tokyoite, such a direct reference to money-making would seem a bit gauche; businesspeople in the capital might instead say 景気はどうですか, which literally means, "How is the economic situation?"

Horiuchi's second statement could be rendered into standard Japanese as いやあ、まあまあですね。私どももうかうかしていられませんよ. The Osaka でんな would be ですな in Tokyo, and the standard *s* in the negative suffix becomes *h*: 〜まへん = 〜ません. Horiuchi's third line corresponds to そうですか。いやあ、困りましたね。うちもぎりぎりなんですよ in Tokyo dialect.

His fourth line can be rendered as つらいですね。山本さんにそう頼まれると。しかしねえ、すんなりはいどうぞ、と言うわけにもいかないでしょう。こちらのつらい立場もわかっていただきたいですね. Here, つろおます means つらいです and ほしおます means ほしいです. Similarly, そない corresponds to そんな（ふう）に and そやけど to そうだけど.

Horiuchi's fifth line becomes the following in Tokyo: それなら結構です。これ以上ずるずる延ばすわけにはいかないでしょうし、値引きさせていただいて、端数をすっぱり切り捨てるということでどうでしょう. Notice that やろ corresponds to だろう or でしょう. The phrase 勉強さしてもろて means 勉強させてもらって, but be careful: 勉強する does not mean "to study" here; the phrase has an additional slang meaning, in both Osaka dialect and standard Japanese, of "to lower the price, to make a discount."

Horiuchi's closing speech, おおきに。あんじょうたのんまっさ, can be rendered as ありがとうございます。よろしくお願いします. The word あんじょう comes from 味良く, meaning "good, well," which, of course, is the origin of よろしく.

The version of Japanese taught to foreigners is nearly always 標準語 *hyōjun-go* "standard Japanese," which is very close to the dialect spoken in the Tokyo area. But as the above conversation shows, people in Osaka speak very differently. In fact, from Hokkaido in the north to Okinawa in the south, Japanese has dozens of distinct dialects, each with its own accent, intonation, and vocabulary. While all Japanese people understand *hyōjun-go*—after all, it is the language of television, radio, and written Japanese—the language they speak in their daily lives varies greatly from region to region. In some areas, such as Tohoku and Kagoshima, the local dialect may be nearly incomprehensible to people from other parts of Japan.

For centuries, the Kansai area, which encompasses Osaka and Kyoto, was the economic and political center of Japan. The distinctive culture and way of life that developed in the region are reflected today in its unique style of speaking. Though it's difficult to convey in writing the full flavor of 大阪弁 *Ōsaka-ben*, here are a few examples:

OSAKA	TOKYO	ENGLISH
ōkini	*arigatō*	thank you
sainara	*sayōnara*	good-bye
gyōsan	*takusan*	many, much
homma	*hontō*	really
omoroi	*omoshiroi*	interesting, fun
donai	*dō, dono yō ni*	how?
wa (both men's and women's speech)	*wa* (women's speech) *yo* (men's speech)	declarative particle

➡ In Japanese, indirect expressions and roundabout ways of talking are often considered more grown-up and sophisticated. This linguistic style appears even in business negotiations, which often proceed without any mention of specific prices or conditions. While this works fine when both parties understand each other, someone who is not used to this type of discussion—particularly a foreigner—may feel confused or even deceived by the lack of concrete information.

The above dialogue between Horiuchi and Yamamoto is a good example. Their conversation is rich with expressions that would be opaque to any outsider:「予算がきちきち」「この間の額」「お支払いはきちんと」「うちもぎりぎり」「端数をすっぱり切り捨てる」「ずばりその線で」。 A phrase used in Yamamoto's second statement—例の件—makes it clear that they have discussed this deal before and that Yamamoto proposed a specific price. Horiuchi is reluctant to accept that price—難儀ですなあ—so Yamamoto urges him to accept the stated conditions. When Yamamoto bows his head, he "stoops to conquer"; rather than putting pressure on the other man, he wants Horiuchi to feel that he would be doing Yamamoto a favor.

Horiuchi shows that he understands Yamamoto's position—つろおますなあ、山本さんにそない言われたら—but by saying そやけどすんなりはいどうぞ、言うわけにもいきまへんやろ。こっちのつらい立場もわかってほしおますなあ, he makes it clear that he won't be able to accept Yamamoto's proposal. Yamamoto shows that he also understands Horiuchi's point of view, but he can't accept it, either—that's the meaning of 困りましたねえ…。 It's at this point that Horiuchi proposes the compromise that closes the deal—端数をすっぱり切り捨てるいうことでどないでっ

しゃろ—but even then the final amount is not mentioned, just that they will "round off the price."

がくんと (gakunto) N / B

To fold, bend, collapse, crack, split, or budge, often because of a sudden shock. Also used to describe a sudden loss of energy or spirit.

❏ 夏休みに遊びすぎたのがたたって*、がくんと成績が落ちちゃったよ。

Natsu-yasumi ni asobisugita no ga tatatte, gakunto seiseki ga ochi-chatta yo.

I got what I deserved for fooling around too much during summer vacation: my grades went into a tailspin.

❀ *Tataru*: to be cursed, ruined, suffer (because of something).

❏ 電車ががくんと急停車したものだから、みんな将棋倒しになっちゃったのよ。

Densha ga gakunto kyū-teisha shita mono da kara, minna shōgi-daoshi ni natchatta no yo.

When the train came lurching to a stop, everyone was knocked flat like a bunch of dominoes (*shōgi* pieces).

ぴりぴり (piripiri) N / B

(1) A sharp feeling of pain, spiciness, electric shock, etc. on the skin, tongue, nose, etc. (2) To become nervous, high-strung, or oversensitive because of fear, unease, tension, etc.

❏ このキムチ、おいしいけど辛いわね。舌にぴりぴりくるわ。

Kono kimuchi, oishii kedo karai wa ne. Shita ni piripiri kuru wa.

This kimchi tastes good, but it sure is spicy. My tongue's on fire.

❏ 子供のいたずらくらいで、そんなにぴりぴり神経をとがらせる*なよ。

Kodomo no itazura kurai de, sonna ni piripiri shinkei o togaraseru na yo.

Don't get so uptight over some kid's prank.

　　※ *Togaraseru*: to sharpen, put on edge.

ぼちぼち／ぽちぽち (bochibochi/pochipochi)　N

(1) Gradually; slowly but steadily. (2) Used to describe something that is about to happen. Imminently. Right away. (3) The condition of many dots or other small objects scattered around. While *bochibochi* and *pochipochi* are nearly identical, *bochibochi* conveys somewhat more emphasis.

❏ 土日を利用してぼちぼち書いてるから、一向に*年賀状、書き終わらないよ。

Donichi o riyō shite bochibochi kaite 'ru kara, ikkō ni nenga-jō, kaki-owaranai yo.

Since I can only plug away at my New Year's cards on the weekends, it seems I'll never finish.

　　※ *Ikkō ni*: (not) at all, (not) a bit.

❏ 雨も上がったし、ぼちぼち出かけようか。

Ame mo agatta shi, bochibochi dekakeyō ka.

The rain's stopped, so let's get going.

❏ このテーブルクロス、ぽちぽちしみがついているから、取り替えましょう。

Kono tēburukurosu, pochipochi shimi ga tsuite iru kara, torikaemashō.

This tablecloth is all stained with spots. Let's change it.

➡ *Nenga-jō* (年賀状) are postcards that people send at the end of each year to their friends, colleagues, and business contacts. While the size of the postcards is standardized, their design and content are not. Many people make their own drawings or prints, often incorporating a picture of the animal that symbolizes the coming year, and the text may vary from a brief formal greeting to a lengthy handwritten message. Parents of small children often attach photos of their offspring.

Most people put their messages on blank cards that are sold each year at the post office. Lottery numbers appear along the bottom of each card, so the people who receive the cards get a chance at winning prizes ranging from a small sheet of stamps to a television or video deck.

Someone with a large circle of acquaintances may send and receive several hundred cards each year. The month of December is thus a busy time as everyone hurries to prepare their New Year's cards. The payback comes on New Year's Day, when the post office makes a special delivery of only New Year's cards, which can be read and enjoyed at leisure through the holidays.

One warning: As a sign of mourning, people who have lost a close relative during the preceding year do not send New Year's cards. Nor does one send a card when this fact is known.

うかうか (ukauka) B
To be careless, absentminded.

❏ すごい人ごみだね。うかうかしていると迷子になりそうだよ。

Sugoi hitogomi da ne. Ukauka shite iru to maigo ni narisō da yo.

What a crowd! You could end up getting lost if you don't watch out.

❏ 来年はもう就職だし、うかうかしてはいられないわ。

Rainen wa mō shūshoku da shi, ukauka shite wa irarenai wa.

I have to look for a job next year, so I can't afford to be fooling around (let things slide) now.

きちきち (kichikichi) N / B

To be full, to have no leeway, to be at the limit.

❏ このおまんじゅう、箱にきちきちに詰まってるわね。

Kono omanjū, hako ni kichikichi ni tsumatte 'ru wa ne.

These *manjū* buns sure are jam-packed into the box.

❏ せっかく海外に行っても、出張じゃスケジュールがきちき
　　ちだからちっとも楽しめないよ。

Sekkaku kaigai ni itte mo, shutchō ja sukejūru ga kichikichi da kara chitto mo tanoshimenai yo.

Now that I've finally gotten a chance to go overseas, it's only a business trip. My schedule is so tight that I won't have any time for fun.

➡ A *manjū* (まんじゅう) is made of a sweet bean paste called あん *an* (or, more informally, あんこ *anko*) that is wrapped in dough and then steamed or roasted. Imported from China by a Buddhist priest in the thirteenth century, the recipe spread throughout Japan in later years and became one of the most popular types of pastry.

きちんと (kichinto) G

Carefully, neatly, accurately, fully, properly.

❏ 布団は、朝起きたらきちんとたたんで押し入れに入れてお
　　いてください。

Futon wa, asa okitara kichinto tatande oshi-ire ni irete oite kudasai.

As soon as you wake up in the morning, fold your futon neatly and put it in the closet.

❏ 伊藤さんはきちんとしているから、待ち合わせに遅れるはずないよ。

Itō-san wa kichinto shite iru kara, machiawase ni okureru hazu nai yo.

Mr. Itō is a very reliable person. I can't see him being late to the meeting.

➡ There are two types of futon in Japan, the *shikibuton* (敷き布団), a relatively thick mattress usually filled with cotton batting, and the *kakebuton* (掛け布団), a lighter quilt filled with cotton, down, wool, polyester, etc. The sleeper lies on the *shikibuton*, which is placed directly on the tatami, floor, or carpet, and the *kakebuton* is used as a blanket.

While beds are becoming more common in Japan, futons retain their popularity because of their convenience. In the morning, they can be folded up and put in the closet, thus freeing the sleeping room for other uses during the day. The closets, called *oshi-ire* (押し入れ), are designed for this purpose, for they typically have a large, flat shelf at about waist height where the futons can be stacked.

ぎりぎり (girigiri) N

With almost no time, space, or leeway to spare. Similar in meaning to *kichikichi*, but *girigiri* emphasizes even more strongly that the ultimate limit has been reached.

❏ ドアが閉まるぎりぎりでかけこみ乗車＊して、けがでもしたらどうするの。

Doa ga shimaru girigiri de kakekomi-jōsha shite, kega de mo shitara dō suru no.

Are you trying to hurt yourself or something, rushing into the train at the very last second like that?

❊ *Kakekomi-jōsha*: rushing onto a train to beat the closing doors.

❏ 給料をもらっても、家のローンを支払っているんで生活費ぎりぎりしか残らないんですよ。

Kyūryō o moratte mo, ie no rōn o shiharatte iru n' de seikatsu-hi giri-giri shika nokoranai n' desu yo.

After paying our home loan, I have barely enough left over from my salary to pay our living expenses.

すんなり (sunnari) G

(1) Slender, smooth, graceful. While *surari* suggests something that is long and straight, *sunnari* emphasizes that the object is also flexible. (2) *Sunnari* is also used to describe something that proceeds smoothly even though some resistance is expected.

❏ 中村さんの指って、すんなりとしていてきれいね。指輪がひきたつわ。

Nakamura-san no yubi tte, sunnari to shite ite kirei ne. Yubiwa ga hiki-tatsu wa.

Your fingers are so nice and slender, Miss Nakamura; they set off your ring very nicely.

❏ もっと高速*が渋滞するかと思ったけど、案外†すんなり通れたね。

Motto kōsoku ga jūtai suru ka to omotta kedo, angai sunnari tōreta ne.

I thought the expressway would be more crowded, but we breezed through without much trouble.

❋ *Kōsoku*: abbreviation of 高速道路 *kōsoku-dōro*.

† *Angai*: surprisingly, unexpectedly.

❏ こっちの言い分をすんなりわかってくれるような人なら、誰も苦労なんかしませんよ。

Kotchi no iibun o sunnari wakatte kureru yō na hito nara, dare mo kurō nanka shimasen yo.

If he could just get what I'm saying through his thick skull, then he wouldn't be such a pain in the neck.

ずるずる (zuruzuru) B

(1) The sound or feeling of a long or heavy object being pulled, dragged, or slid. (2) The sound or appearance of slurping, snuffling, sniffing—that is, inhaling a wet object or substance (soba noodles, mucus, etc.). (3) To slip, fall, collapse; to be unable to maintain a fixed position. (4) To dawdle, to let a bad situation drag on, to be unable to reach a satisfactory conclusion. Except when used to describe noodle eating, *zuruzuru* generally has a negative connotation of slackness or laziness.

❑ 靴ひもをずるずる引きずって歩いていると、危ないですよ。

Kutsuhimo o zuruzuru hikizutte aruite iru to, abunai desu yo.

It's dangerous to walk around dragging your shoelaces like that.

❑ 鼻をずるずるすすっていないで、ちゃんとかみなさい。

Hana o zuruzuru susutte inai de, chanto kaminasai.

Stop all that sniffling and blow your nose.

❑ この靴下、ずるずるずり落ちて困るんだ。

Kono kutsushita, zuruzuru zuriochite komaru n' da.

I hate these socks because they keep sliding down.

❏ すぐ失礼するつもりだったんですけど、ついずるずる長居[❋]
をしてしまってすみません。

*Sugu shitsurei suru tsumori datta n' desu kedo, tsui zuruzuru nagai o
shite shimatte sumimasen.*

I'm afraid I've worn out my welcome. I hadn't intended to stay so
long.

> ❋ *Nagai*: an unconscionably long visit.

すっぱり (suppari) G / N

(1) To cut, break, or separate sharply and neatly. (2) To arrange a matter decisively and permanently so that nothing undone remains. Used
particularly when quitting or giving something up.

❏ 植木屋さんが枝をすっぱり払ってくれたのはいいけど、何
だか寒々としちゃったわね。

*Uekiya-san ga eda o suppari haratte kureta no wa ii kedo, nan da ka
samuzamu to shichatta wa ne.*

True, the gardener cut back the branches very nicely, but now the
tree looks so forlorn.

❏ 胃かいようを患ってから、酒はすっぱりやめたんだ。

I-kaiyō o wazuratte kara, sake wa suppari yameta n' da.

I went cold turkey on the alcohol after I got an ulcer.

ずばり (zubari) G / N

(1) To cut, slice, or strike something with a single sharp blow. While
suppari suggests that the object is completely severed, *zubari* can be
used even when the cut is not complete. Often *zubari* emphasizes the
accuracy of the action. (2) To go to the core of a subject, to be right on

target. Often used to describe a plain, direct manner of speaking that gets straight to the point or an insight that reveals a hidden truth.

___

❏ 剣道はやはりこわいですよ。一瞬のすきを、ずばり打ちこまれますからね。

Kendō wa yahari kowai desu yo. Isshun no suki o, zubari uchikomaremasu kara ne.

I think kendō is really scary. Give your opponent the slightest opening and he'll score a hit.

❏ あそこの占いはずばりと当たるって評判なのよ。

Asoko no uranai wa zubari to ataru tte hyōban na no yo.

They say that fortune-teller is always right on the money.

Quiz

Fill in the blanks with one of the words studied in this chapter: が
くんと gakunto, ぴりぴり piripiri, ぼちぼち／ぽちぽち bochi-
bochi/pochipochi, うかうか ukauka, きちきち kichikichi, きちんと
kichinto, ぎりぎり girigiri, すんなり sunnari, ずるずる zuruzuru,
すっぱり suppari, ずばり zubari. There are at least two sentences for
each word. Answers are on page 217.

1 お隣のご主人、奥さんが亡くなってから、(　　　　　) 老けこ
んじゃったわね。

*Otonari no go-shujin, okusan ga nakunatte kara, (　　　　) fukekon-
jatta wa ne.*

Since his wife passed away, the man next-door has suddenly aged.

2 何を (　　　　　) しているんだ。少しは気を抜いたらどうだ。

Nani o (　　　　) shite iru n' da. Sukoshi wa ki o nuitara dō da.

What're you so on edge about? How 'bout easing off a bit.

3 あの子、顔に (　　　　　) そばかすがあって、可愛かったね。

Ano ko, kao ni (　　　　) sobakasu ga atte, kawaikatta ne.

He was really cute with those freckles on his face.

4 電車がすごい混雑で、(　　　　　)してたら乗り過ごしてしまった。

Densha ga sugoi konzatsu de, (　　　　　) shite 'tara norisugoshite shi-matta.

The train was packed to the ceiling, and I missed my stop when my mind drifted off someplace.

5 冷蔵庫は(　　　　　)に詰まっていてもう何も入らないわ。

Reizōko wa (　　　　　) ni tsumatte ite mō nani mo hairanai wa.

The refrigerator is so stuffed with things there isn't room for any more.

6 洗濯物は(　　　　　)たたみましょう。

Sentakumono wa (　　　　　) tatamimashō.

Let's fold the laundry nice and neat.

7 人数分(　　　　　)しか、いすがないんだ。

Ninzūbun (　　　　　) shika, isu ga nai n' da.

There are only enough chairs for a fixed number of people.

8 (　　　　　)と話がまとまるといいけれど。

(　　　　　) to hanashi ga matomaru to ii keredo.

I hope everything works out smoothly.

9 いつまでも(　　　　　)と返事を延ばすのは迷惑だ。

Itsu made mo (　　　　　) to henji o nobasu no wa meiwaku da.

It causes all kinds of trouble to have the answer continually put off.

10 シェフは大根の葉を（　　　　）切り落としました。

Shefu wa daikon no ha o (　　　　) kiriotoshimashita.

The chef cleanly cut off the daikon leaves.

11 相手の思惑を（　　　　）と見事に見抜きましたね。

Aite no omowaku o (　　　) to migoto ni minukimashita ne.

She saw right through what the other party was thinking.

12 スピードが（　　　　）落ちたのは、エンジンのせいだ。

Supīdo ga (　　　) ochita no wa, enjin no sei da.

It was the engine that caused the dramatic drop in speed.

13 ぬれた手でプリンターに触れたら（　　　　）したよ。危なかったね。

Nureta te de purintā ni furetara (　　　) shita yo. Abunakatta ne.

When I touched the printer with my wet hands, I got a sudden shock. That was a close one.

14 だいたいメンバーもそろったみたいだから、（　　　　）始めようか。

Daitai menbā mo sorotta mitai da kara, (　　　　) hajimeyō ka.

It looks like everyone's here. Shall we start getting down to work?

15 こう競争が激しいと、こっちも（　　　　）していられないね。

Kō kyōsō ga hageshii to, kotchi mo (　　　) shite irarenai ne.

With competition as tough as this, we just can't stand around like statues.

16 明日も早いから、(　　　　　)寝るとしようか。

Ashita mo hayai kara, (　　　　　) neru to shiyō ka.

We've got to get up early again tomorrow, so maybe it's time to hit
　　　the sack.

17 このズボンは僕にはもう(　　　　　)ではけないよ。

Kono zubon wa boku ni wa mō (　　　　　) de hakenai yo.

These trousers are so tight I can't get them on anymore.

18 彼は真面目だから約束は(　　　　)守るでしょう。

Kare wa majime da kara yakusoku wa (　　　　) mamoru deshō.

He is very serious, so he's bound to keep his promise.

19 (　　　　　)のところで、始業時刻に間に合った。

(　　　　　) no tokoro de, shigyō-jikoku ni ma ni atta.

I arrived in the nick of time, just before starting time.

20 (　　　　　)とした足で、本当にスタイルのいい人ですね。

(　　　　　) to shita ashi de, hontō ni sutairu no ii hitro desu ne.

With such long, slender legs, she's got a really good figure.

21 花粉症だから、人前でも(　　　　)鼻水が出てきて困っちゃ
うんだ。

Kafun-shō da kara, hitomae de mo (　　　　) hanamizu ga dete kite
　　　komatchau n' da.

I have hay fever, and I get a runny nose right in front of people. It's
　　　really embarrassing.

QUIZ

22 彼女のことは（　　　　）あきらめます。

Kanojo no koto wa (　　　　) akiramemasu.

I'm just going to give up on her in one clean break.

23 （　　　　）当ててみましょうか。

（　　　　） *atete mimashō ka.*

Now, just let me guess.

A MAN'S PLACE

Mari Wakabayashi and Harumi Yamato are nodding acquaintances at their fitness club. They have a chat as they work out on exercise machines.

A MAN'S PLACE

大和 「**こんがり**焼けていらっしゃいますね。海ですか。」

若林 「ええ、プーケットに行ってきたんです。焼き過ぎてまだ**ひりひり***しちゃって。」

大和 「いいですね。ご主人とご一緒に？」

若林 「ええまあ。」

大和 「うらやましいわ。うちなんか、夏休みも結局家で**ごろごろ**しているだけ。近頃**ぶくぶく**太ってきちゃって。それにしても、ご精が出ます†ね。」

若林 「トライアスロンをやっているものですから。」

大和 「えっ、あの鉄人レースの？すごいわあ。」

若林 「すごくないんですよ。ジョギングから始めて、**じりじり**と距離を伸ばしていって…。**こつこつ**練習すれば、誰にでもできますよ。」

大和 「じゃあ、プーケットでも、トレーニングを？」

若林 「もちろん。」

大和 「道理で*＊**すらりと**していらっしゃると思ったわ。ご主人もやっぱり？」

若林 「いいえ、うちのは**ずんぐりむっくり**の純日本型。学生時代は相撲部ですもの。」

大和 「まあ、**がっしり**していていいじゃありませんの。トレーニングにも付き合ってくださるんでしょう？」

若林 「まさか。機内では**ぐっすり**、ホテルでは**ぐったり**、海辺では**ごろごろ**していただけですわ。」

* *Hirihiri:* see "Feeling Out of Sorts?" (p. 110).
† *Sei ga deru:* energy comes forth; to be energetic.
❖ *Dōri de:* with reason; it stands to reason; no wonder.

Yamato:	*Kongari yakete irasshaimasu ne. Umi desu ka.*
Wakabayashi:	*Ē, Pūketto ni itte kita n' desu. Yakisugite mada hirihiri shichatte.*
Yamato:	*Ii desu ne. Goshujin to go-issho ni?*
Wakabayashi:	*Ē mā.*
Yamato:	*Urayamashii wa. Uchi nanka, natsu-yasumi mo kekkyoku ie de gorogoro shite 'ru dake. Chikagoro bukubuku futotte kichatte. Sore ni shite mo, go-sei ga demasu ne.*
Wakabayashi:	*Toraiasuron o yatte iru mono desu kara.*
Yamato:	*E—, ano tetsujin-rēsu no? Sugoi wā.*
Wakabayashi:	*Sugoku nai n' desu yo. Jogingu kara hajimete, jirijiri to kyori o nobashite itte… Kotsukotsu renshū sureba, dare ni de mo dekimasu yo.*
Yamato:	*Jā, Pūketto de mo, torēningu o?*
Wakabayashi:	*Mochiron.*
Yamato:	*Dōri de surarito shite irassharu to omotta wa. Goshujin mo yappari?*
Wakabayashi:	*Īe, uchi no wa zunguri-mukkuri no jun–Nihon-gata. Gakusei-jidai wa sumō-bu desu mono.*
Yamato:	*Mā, gasshiri shite ite ii ja arimasen no. Torēningu ni mo tsukiatte kudasaru n' deshō?*
Wakabayashi:	*Masaka. Kinai de wa gussuri, hoteru de wa guttari, umibe de wa gorogoro shite ita dake desu wa.*

$$\text{\small ✴ ✴ ✴}$$

Yamato: What a lovely copper tan you have! Did you go to the beach?

Wakabayashi: Yes, I just came back from Phuket (Thailand). I got a sunburn, and it still stings.

Yamato: Wow, Phuket. Did you go with your husband?

Wakabayashi: Well, yes, as a matter of fact.

Yamato: I'm so envious. All my husband does is lie around the house, even during his summer vacation. Lately he's been putting on weight, too. But, hey, you're getting quite a workout.

Wakabayashi: You see, I do triathlons.

Yamato: What, you mean those iron-man races? That's amazing!

Wakabayashi: There's nothing amazing about it. I just started by jogging, and little by little built up to longer distances. Anyone can do it—you just have to keep plugging away.

Yamato: Did you train when you were at Phuket, too?

Wakabayashi: Of course.

Yamato: I *thought* you looked so nice and slim. Your husband's the same, I suppose.

Wakabayashi: Not at all. He's a typical dumpy Japanese guy. In fact, he was on the sumo team in college.

Yamato: Well, it must be nice to have a solid, well-built man. I suppose he goes along when you're training.

Wakabayashi: Ha! That's a laugh. He conked out on the airplane, pooped out at the hotel, and stretched out when we got to the beach.

こんがり (kongari) G

To be burned or toasted to a pleasant, golden brown.

❏ トーストはこんがりきつね色になるまで焼いてね。

Tōsuto wa kongari kitsune-iro ni naru made yaite ne.

Toast the bread until it's a nice, light brown, all right?

❏ 夏はやっぱりこんがりと小麦色に焼けた肌が魅力的だね。

Natsu wa yappari kongari to komugi-iro ni yaketa hada ga miryoku-teki da ne.

A nice, coffee-brown tan really does look great in summer.

ごろごろ (gorogoro) N / B

(1) The sound or fact of some large, bulky object, animal, or person rolling or tumbling over. *Gorogoro* can also refer to many such objects in confused disarray (N). (2) To spend time doing nothing—includes the image of a person lolling in a recumbent position (N/B).

❏ 引っ越しって本当に大変ね、うちなんかまだダンボールが ごろごろ転がったままよ。

Hikkoshi tte hontō ni taihen ne, uchi nanka mada danbōru ga goro-goro korogatta mama yo.

Moving is a real pain. We still have cardboard boxes scattered all over the house.

❏「落石注意」と書かれていても、実際にごろごろ岩が落ち
　てきたらひとたまりもない*ね。

*Rakuseki chūi" to kakarete ite mo, jissai ni gorogoro iwa ga ochite
kitara hito-tamari mo nai ne.*

The sign says "Watch for Falling Rocks," but if boulders really
started tumbling down, there wouldn't be much you could do
(you'd be a goner).

> ❀ *Hito-tamari mo nai*: not be able to withstand something for even a short time
> (*hito-tamari*, lit. "a single puddle").

❏ 休みの日は思いきり朝寝坊して、一日中家でごろごろして
　いるのが最高だね。

*Yasumi no hi wa omoikiri asa-nebō shite, ichinichi-jū ie de gorogoro
shite iru no ga saikō da ne.*

My favorite way to spend a day off is to sleep as late as I can in the
morning and then spend the rest of the day lounging around
the house.

❏ いい若い者が、いつまでごろごろ寝ているんですか。

Ii wakai mono ga, itsu made gorogoro nete iru n' desu ka.

How long do you plan to stay sacked out like this, a healthy young
fellow like you?

ぶくぶく (bukubuku) B

Fat, swollen, puffy; said of the human body due to an excess of fat,
fluid, or clothing.

❏ 結婚したら急にぶくぶくと太り出しちゃって、みんなに冷
　やかされるんです。

Kekkon shitara kyū ni bukubuku to futoridashichatte, minna ni hiya-kasareru n' desu.

Everyone kids me because I plumped out soon after I got married.

❑ 冬のラッシュはいやですね。みんなぶくぶくに着ぶくれ*
　して身動きもできません。

Fuyu no rasshu wa iya desu ne. Minna bukubuku ni kibukure shite miugoki mo dekimasen.

I hate the train during rush hour in winter. With all the bulky clothes everyone is wearing, you can hardly move.

　　❊ *Kibukure*: from *kiru* (to wear) and *fukureu* (to swell).

じりじり (jirijiri) N

(1) To move or advance slowly but steadily in a certain direction.
(2) Bright, direct, scorching sunlight.

❑ このところじりじり物価が上がっているから、生活費がか
　さんで困るわ。

Kono tokoro jirijiri bukka ga agatte iru kara, seikatsu-hi ga kasande komaru wa.

The way prices keep climbing, I'm feeling the pinch in my living expenses.

❑ まだ5月なのに、沖縄は太陽がじりじり照りつけてまるで
　真夏のようだったよ。

Mada gogatsu na no ni, Okinawa wa taiyō ga jirijiri teritsukete maru de manatsu no yō datta yo.

In Okinawa the sun was beating down so hard that it felt practically like midsummer, though it was still only May.

こつこつ (kotsukotsu) G

To do something slowly but surely, without flash or ostentation.
Often used in a positive sense to describe steady, continuous effort.

❑ 兄はひらめき型、弟はこつこつ型なんだが、僕は困ったこ
とにどっちでもないんだ。

*Ani wa hirameki-gata, otōto wa kotsukotsu-gata nan da ga, boku wa
komatta koto ni dotchi de mo nai n' da.*

My big brother is a real brain, and my little brother is the slow-but-
steady type. My problem is that I'm neither one nor the other.

❑ こつこつと勉強するのがどうも苦手で、いつも一夜漬けに
なっちゃうんです。

*Kotsukotsu to benkyō suru no ga dōmo nigate de, itsumo ichiya-zuke
ni natchau n' desu.*

I'm no good at keeping up with my studies. I always wind up pulling
an all-nighter.

すらりと (surarito) G

Slim, svelte, slender. Often used to describe thin, attractive bodies,
arms, legs, etc.

❑ マイケルってかっこいいのよ。すらりと背が高くてね。

Maikeru tte kakko ii no yo. Surarito se ga takakute ne.

Michael is one cool-looking guy. So tall and slender and all.

❑ すらりと伸びた足さえあれば、ミニスカートをはけるんだ
けど。

Surarito nobita ashi sae areba, mini-sukāto o hakeru n' da kedo.

If only my legs were nice and long and slim, I could wear a mini-
skirt, too.

ずんぐりむっくり／ずんぐり (zunguri-mukkuri/zunguri) N / B

Short and fat, dumpy, stout, portly. *Zunguri-mukkuri* is more
emphatic.

❏ この大根は、ずんぐりしていて見栄え*は悪いけど、すご
くおいしいよ。

Kono daikon wa, zunguri shite ite mibae wa warui kedo, sugoku oishii yo.

This giant radish doesn't look like much, all bloated up the way it is,
but it tastes great.

❈ *Mibae*: outward appearance (positive unless with negative qualifier).

❏ 道産子はサラブレッドと違ってずんぐりむっくりだけど、
馬力があるんだよ。

*Dosan-ko wa sarabureddo to chigatte zunguri-mukkuri da kedo, bariki
ga aru n' da.*

Hokkaido-bred horses are much stockier than thoroughbreds, but
they've got a lot of power.

がっしり (gasshiri) G

Strong, solidly built, rugged, muscular.

❏ 男の人はやっぱりがっしりしていないとね。

Otoko no hito wa yappari gasshiri shite inai to ne.

A man's no good if he's not a hunk. (I like a man who's really solidly
built.)

❑ 古い家なんですけどがっしりできているんで、まだ壊すに
はちょっともったいないんです。

*Furui ie nan desu kedo gasshiri dekite iru n' de, mada kowasu ni wa
chotto mottainai n' desu.*

This house is old but it's as solid as a rock. It would be a shame to
tear it down now.

ぐっすり (gussuri) G / N

To sleep soundly, to be fast asleep.

❑ 夕べはぐっすり寝ていたから、地震があったなんて全然知
らなかったなあ。

*Yūbe wa gussuri nete ita kara, jishin ga atta nan te zenzen shira-
nakatta nā.*

I was sleeping like a log last night, so I had no idea there was an
earthquake.

❑ 風邪薬を飲んでぐっすり眠ったら、頭痛がとれたわ。

Kaze-gusuri o nonde gussuri nemuttara, zutsū ga toreta wa.

I got rid of my headache by taking some cold medicine and getting a
good night's sleep.

ぐったり (guttari) B

To be tired, droopy, or desiccated because of fatigue, illness, dehy-
dration, disappointment, etc. Usually used to describe people, animals, or plants.

❑ 田舎に帰ったのはいいけど、まいったよ。帰省*ラッシュ
で着いた頃にはもうぐったりさ。

*Inaka ni kaetta no wa ii kedo, maitta yo. Kisei-rasshu de tsuita koro ni
wa mō guttari sa.*

It was nice getting back to my hometown again, but the going-home rush was a bitch. By the time I got there I was completely wiped out.

❊ *Kisei*: lit., "to return and inquire (as to the health of one's parents)"; to return to one's home outside the big city.

❏ あまりの暑さに、庭の花までぐったりしおれているわ。

Amari no atsusa ni, niwa no hana made guttari shiorete iru wa.

It's so hot, even the flowers in the garden are wilting (going limp).

➥ *Kisei-rasshu* (帰省ラッシュ) refers to the mass movement of people from Tokyo and other big cities back to their hometowns during the Obon and New Year's holiday seasons. Trains and airplanes are packed, and traffic jams on expressways can stretch for a hundred kilometers or more.

The word "Obon" comes from the 盂蘭盆会 *Urabon-e*, or Bon Festival, which is based on the Buddhist text 盂蘭盆経 *Urabon-kyō*, or *Ullambana Sutra*. The original purpose of the festival was to comfort the spirits of the dead, and in fact many Japanese still choose this occasion to visit the graves of their ancestors. Less ghostly customs have become associated with the festival as well, including 盆踊り *bon odori*, the folk dances performed in the summer evening in nearly every town, village, and neighborhood in Japan. Obon is celebrated in mid July in some areas and mid August in others, but the peak of the *kisei-rasshu* comes around August 15, and stores often close for a few days then. A similar rush to the countryside to visit relatives occurs at New Year's, for most people have at least January 1, 2, and 3 as holidays.

Quiz

Fill in the blanks with one of the words studied in this chapter: こんがり kongari, ごろごろ gorogoro, ぶくぶく bukubuku, じりじり jirijiri, こつこつ kotsukotsu, すらりと surarito, ずんぐりむっくり／ずんぐり zunguri-mukkuri/zunguri, がっしり gasshiri, ぐっすり gussuri, ぐったり guttari. There are at least two sentences for each word. Answers are on page 218.

1 (　　　　)と健康的に焼けているね。ゴルフにでも行ったの？

(　　　　) to kenkō-teki ni yakete iru ne. Gorufu ni de mo itta no?

You sure have a nice golden tan. Did you go golfing or something?

2 定年で会社を辞めてから、うちで(　　　　)しているんだ。

Teinen de kaisha o yamete kara, uchi de (　　　　) shite iru n' da.

Since leaving the company after retirement, I've been lounging around the house doing nothing.

3 みんな(　　　　)に着込んでいるから、込んだ電車の中では身動きもできないよ。

Minna (　　　　) ni kikonde iru kara, konda densha no naka de wa miugoki mo dekinai yo.

Everyone is so bundled up on the train that you can hardly move.

4 台風で川の水位が（　　　　　）と上がってきています。

Taifū de kawa no suii ga (　　　　) to agatte kite imasu.

Because of the typhoon, the water level in the river is gradually rising.

5 （　　　　　）ためてきたお金を元手に商売を始めたんだ。

（　　　　） *tamete kita okane o motode ni shōbai o hajimeta n' da.*

I've started my own business using my hard-earned savings as capital.

6 この服は背が高くて（　　　　）した人が似合う服だね。

Kono fuku wa se ga takakute (　　　　) shita hito ga niau fuku da ne.

These clothes would suit someone who is tall and slender.

7 子供のときは（　　　　）だったんだけど、中学に入ってから急に背が伸びたんだ。

Kodomo no toki wa (　　　　) datta n' da kedo, chūgaku ni haitte kara kyū ni se ga nobita n' da.

As a child he was short and dumpy, but he suddenly shot up in junior high.

8 家はやっぱり骨組みが（　　　　）していないと。

Ie wa yappari honegumi ga (　　　　) shite inai to.

A house should have a sturdy framework.

9 （　　　　　）眠っていたので物音に気づきませんでした。

（　　　　） *nemutte ita no de monooto ni kizukimasen deshita.*

I was sleeping soundly, so I didn't notice the noise.

10 遊園地に行ったのはいいけど、子供たちは帰りには疲れて（　　　　）してたね。

Yūen-chi ni itta no wa ii kedo, kodomo-tachi wa kaeri ni wa tsukarete ( ) *shite 'ta ne.*

Going to the amusement park was okay, but the kids got tired on the way back and went as limp as noodles.

11 ( ) 焼けたトーストにおいしい紅茶、それが私の朝食です。

( ) *yaketa tōsuto ni oishii kōcha, sore ga watashi no chōshoku desu.*

A piece of golden-brown toast and a cup of tea—that's my breakfast.

12 じゃがいもをたくさんもらったので、床に( )置いてあるんだ。

Jagaimo o takusan moratta no de, yuka ni ( ) *oite aru n' da.*

I got a bunch of potatoes and left them lying on the floor.

13 昔はやせてたんだけど、30歳過ぎたら( )太りだしちゃったんだ。

Mukashi wa yasete ita n' da kedo, sanjū sugitara ( ) *futori-dashichatta n' da.*

I used to be slim, but after turning thirty I started to balloon up.

14 浜辺では( )と太陽が照り付けて暑かったよ。

Hamabe de wa ( ) *to taiyō ga teritsukete atsukatta yo.*

What with the sun beating down on the beach, it was really hot.

15 長年( )と研究してきた成果が認められてよかったね。

Naganen ( ) *to kenkyū shite kita seika ga mitomerarete yokatta ne.*

It's great that your steady research over the years has been recognized.

16 ダイエットの効果かな、ずいぶん（　　　　）したね。

Daietto no kōka ka na, zuibun (　　　　) shita ne.

Maybe it's the diet; she sure looks nice and slim.

17 兄は（　　　　）した小太りの体型だし、弟は背が高くて、兄弟でも全然似ていないんだ。

Ani wa (　　　　) shita kobutori no taikei da shi, otōto wa se ga takakute, kyōdai de mo zenzen nite inai n' da.

The older brother is short and dumpy, and the younger one is tall. Even though they're brothers, they don't look alike at all.

18 あの人、（　　　　）しているけど、何かスポーツでもやっていたのかな。

Ano hito, (　　　　) shite iru kedo, nani ka supōtsu de mo yatte ita no ka na.

He is really well built. Did he play some kind of sports?

19 今晩は（　　　　）おやすみなさい。

Konban wa (　　　　) oyasumi nasai.

Tonight, try to get a good night's sleep.

20 3日間も徹夜したので、もう（　　　　）だよ。

Mikka-kan mo tetsuya shita no de, mō (　　　　) da yo.

I've pulled three all-nighters in a row. I'm completely wiped out.

A BIG HEADACHE

M akoto Saitō, an employee of Taishō Bank, has been drowsy all morning. His coworker Shigeo Suzuki detects evidence of a hangover.

A BIG HEADACHE

鈴木　「うかない*顔ですね。」

斉藤　「いやあ†、まいりました。」

鈴木　(手で口元にお猪口を持っていく動作をして)「コレですか。」

斉藤　「支店長とね。朝起きたら、頭は**がんがん**、胃は**むかむか**。」

鈴木　「つらいですよね。」

斉藤　「起き上がろうとしたら、もう**くらくら**しちゃって。」

鈴木　「わかります、わかります。そういうときに、会議で**くどく
　　　　ど**部長のお説教を聞かされると、こたえるんですよね。」

斉藤　「**げんなり**ですね。しかし、夕べは変だなあ。**べろべろ**に
　　　　なるまで飲んだわけでもないのに。年かなあ。」

鈴木　「普段**ばりばり**やっている分、ストレスがたまってたん
　　　　じゃないですか。」

斉藤　「支店長も**ぐいぐい**コップ酒でいっちゃって。最後にはカ
　　　　ウンターで**うつらうつら**ですよ。」

鈴木　「それじゃあ、支店長を送っていったんですか。」

斉藤　「そうそう。何しろ*たっぷり1時間は乗りますからね。
　　　　ぼくもタクシーの中でつい*うとうとしちゃって。」

鈴木　「大変でしたね。」

斉藤　「ええ、まあ。あっ、大変だ。」

鈴木　「何ですか、急に。」

斉藤　「**うっかり**タクシー代の領収書をもらうのを忘れた！」

❃ *Ukanai*: lit., "not floating"; downcast, crestfallen.
† *Iyā*: an exclamation expressing surprise, embarrassment, etc.
❖ *Nani shiro*: in any case, anyhow; emphasizing what follows.
✿ *Tsui*: in the end, before realizing it.

Suzuki: *Ukanai kao desu ne.*

Saitō: *Iyā, mairimashita.*

Suzuki: (te de kuchimoto ni ochoko o motte iku dōsa o shite): *Kore desu ka.*

Saitō: *Shiten-chō to ne. Asa okitara, atama wa gangan, i wa muka-muka.*

Suzuki: *Tsurai desu yo ne.*

Saitō: *Okiagarō to shitara, mō kurakura shichatte.*

Suzuki: *Wakarimasu, wakarimasu. Sō iu toki ni, kaigi de kudokudo buchō no osekkyō o kikasareru to, kotaeru n' desu yo ne.*

Saitō: *Gennari desu ne. Shikashi, yūbe wa hen da nā. Berobero ni naru made nonda wake de mo nai no ni. Toshi ka nā.*

Suzuki: *Fudan baribari yatte iru bun, sutoresu ga tamatte 'ta n' ja nai desu ka.*

Saitō: *Shiten-chō mo guigui koppu-zake de itchatte. Saigo ni wa kauntā de utsura-utsura desu yo.*

Suzuki: *Sore jā, shiten-chō o okutte itta n' desu ka.*

Saitō: *Sō sō. Nani shiro tappuri ichi-jikan wa norimasu kara ne. Boku mo takushī no naka de tsui utouto shichatte.*

Suzuki: *Taihen deshita ne.*

Saitō: *Ē, mā. A——, taihen da.*

Suzuki: *Nan desu ka, kyū ni.*

Saitō: *Ukkari takushī-dai no ryōshū-sho o morau no o wasureta!*

＊　＊　＊

Suzuki:	You really look down in the dumps today.
Saitō:	Yeah, it's the pits all right.
Suzuki:	(cupping one hand and raising it to his mouth as if to drink from a sake cup) Is this the problem?
Saitō:	Yeah, I was out with the branch manager. This morning I woke up to a pounding headache and a churning stomach.
Suzuki:	That's too bad.
Saitō:	When I tried to get up, I felt sort of woozy.
Suzuki:	I know what you mean. And then if you've got to listen to the division chief give one of his sermons at a meeting, it can be pretty tough.
Saitō:	Yeah, I'm sick of it. Last night was funny, though. I didn't drink myself under the table or anything. Maybe I'm getting old.
Suzuki:	You always put so much into your work (work your tail off), maybe the stress is getting to you.
Saitō:	The branch manager was drinking sake from a glass and really guzzling it down. Near the end he nodded off right there at the counter.
Suzuki:	So you had to see him home?
Saitō:	That's right. Anyhow, it took a solid hour to get home. I ended up conking out (nodding off) in the cab myself.
Suzuki:	Sounds tough.
Saitō:	Yeah, well…. Uh-oh, now I've blown it.
Suzuki:	What's the matter?
Saitō:	The taxi fare! I completely forgot to get a receipt.

➥ Sake is usually poured from a small earthenware bottle called a 徳利 *tokkuri* into a small cup called an お猪口 *ochoko* or 杯 *sakazuki* or into a slightly larger vessel called a ぐい飲み *guinomi*. The cupping of the right hand as if holding an *ochoko* and bringing it near the mouth is simple sign language for drinking sake.

While drinkers usually sip sake slowly from an *ochoko* or *guinomi*, when they want to proceed at a fast pace they drink from a small glass called a コップ *koppu*, hence コップ酒 *koppu-zake* (often sold in vending machines in a small cuplike bottle). (Note that *koppu*, taken from the Dutch word *kop*, means "a glass," while カップ *kappu*, from the English "cup," means just that: "a cup.")

むかむか (mukamuka) B

To feel woozy, nauseous. Or to be so discomforted, angry, etc. that you feel like throwing up.

❏ 乗り物酔いかしら、なんだかむかむかしてきたわ。

Norimono-yoi kashira, nan da ka mukamuka shite kita wa.

Maybe I'm getting carsick. I think I'm going to throw up.

❏ きのうの課長の言い草、思い出しただけでもむかむかするね。

Kinō no kachō no iigusa, omoidashita dake de mo mukamuka suru ne.

Just thinking about the way the section chief talked yesterday is enough to make you puke (make you sick to your stomach).

くらくら (kurakura) N

To feel dizzy, shaky, unsteady on one's feet.

❏ 頭がくらくらするんだけど、血圧でも高いのかしら。

Atama ga kurakura suru n' da kedo, ketsuatsu de mo takai no kashira.

My head seems to be spinning. I wonder if I might have high blood pressure or something.

□ 転勤を言いわたされたときには、一瞬＊くらくらきたよ。

Tenkin o iiwatasareta toki ni wa, isshun kurakura kita yo.

When they told me I was going to be transferred, you could have knocked me over with a feather.

    ❁ *Isshun*: (for) an instant.

くどくど (kudokudo) B

To say the same thing over and over again. Often used to describe annoying long-windedness.

□ くどくどと言い訳したところで、物事何も進展しないよ。

Kudokudo to iiwake shita tokoro de, monogoto nani mo shinten shinai yo.

Nothing is going to be accomplished by your going on and on making excuses.

□ 年のせい＊か母も愚痴っぽくなって†ね、会うたびにくどくど聞かされるんで弱っちゃう❖よ。

Toshi no sei ka haha mo guchippoku natte ne, au tabi ni kudokudo kikasareru n' de yowatchau yo.

My mother's really turned into a complainer in her old age. Every time I see her, she nearly talks me to death.

    ❁ *Sei*: on account of.

    † *Guchippoi*: complaining (*guchi* "complaints" + the adjective-forming *ppoi*).

    ❖ *Yowaru*: lit., "weakened"; at a loss, flummoxed.

げんなり (gennari) B

To feel exhausted, beat, worn out, burned out, disgusted. While *unzari* expresses mental exhaustion or disgust, *gennari* describes a lack of energy that is both mental and physical.

❑ けさったら*、事故で2時間も満員電車に閉じ込められたんだぜ。もうげんなりだよ。

Kesa ttara, jiko de ni-jikan mo man'in-densha ni tojikomerareta n' da ze. Mō gennari da yo.

This morning—would you believe it—there was this accident, and I was trapped in a crowded train for two solid hours. I've had it up to here.

> ❊ *Ttara*: introduces a subject with a modicum of criticism, denigration, or intimacy. Used in a colloquial context.

❑ 決算期にはくる日もくる日も数字とにらめっこ*で、いいかげん†げんなりするよ。

Kessan-ki ni wa kuru hi mo kuru hi mo sūji to niramekko de, ii kagen gennari suru yo.

When we're closing the books, I spend day after day staring at numbers. I'm fed up with it.

> ❊ *Niramekko*: outstaring or staring down.

> † *Ii kagen*: originally, the proper amount or degree; here, colloquial for "pretty much, considerably."

べろべろ (berobero) B

(1) To stick out one's tongue in an exaggerated manner and lick something repeatedly. (2) To be drunk to the point of physical impairment.

❑ 犬に顔をべろべろなめられて、くすぐったかったわ。

Inu ni kao o berobero namerarete, kusuguttakatta wa.

This dog licked me all over the face. My, did it tickle!

❑ 夕べはべろべろに酔っぱらって帰ってきたけど、何かいやなことでもあったの。

Yūbe wa berobero ni yopparatte kaette kita kedo, nani ka iya na koto de mo atta no.

You were drunk as a skunk when you got home last night. What was the matter?

ばりばり (baribari) G / N

(1) The sound of something being ripped, torn, scratched, struck, or crunched (N). (2) To do something steadily, energetically. Often used to describe a person who works hard and enthusiastically (G/N). (3) Stiff, rigid (N).

❑ ごませんべいをばりばり食べながら、相撲をテレビで見るのが土日の楽しみなんだ。

Goma-senbei o baribari tabenagara, sumō o terebi de miru no ga donichi no tanoshimi nan da.

Munching on sesame crackers while watching sumo on TV—that's how I like to spend my weekends.

❑ あいかわらず、彼女はばりばり仕事をしているよ。

Aikawarazu, kanojo wa baribari shigoto o shite iru yo.

She's still going full throttle at her work. Hasn't changed one bit.

❑ 寺沢さんは、現役*ばりばりの政治記者だから、お忙しいんじゃないですか。

Terasawa-san wa, gen'eki baribari no seiji-kisha da kara, oisogashii n' ja nai desu ka.

As a political journalist at the peak of his career, Mr. Terasawa must be terribly busy.

✤ *Gen'eki*: on active duty; active (not retired or out of the mainstream).

❏ タオルを外に干しておいたら、ばりばりに凍っちゃったわ。

Taoru o soto ni hoshite oitara, baribari ni kōtchatta wa.

The towels froze and got all crackly when I hung them out to dry.

➡ *Sembei* are roasted crackers made from rice or wheat flour and flavored with soy sauce, salt, sugar, and other ingredients. *Goma sembei* contain soy sauce and sesame seeds.

While sumo ranks a distant second to baseball among spectator sports in Japan, it does enjoy a steady popularity. Six fifteen-day tournaments are held each year, and all are broadcast by NHK, the public television and radio network.

ぐいぐい (guigui) G / N

(1) To drink sake or another liquid quickly and vigorously. The word is used positively to denote a lively, enthusiastic style of drinking. (2) To push or pull strongly or steadily. To do something with energy or vigor.

❏ 夏は冷えたビールをぐいぐい飲むのが最高ですね。

Natsu wa hieta bīru o guigui nomu no ga saikō desu ne.

When summer comes around, there's nothing like chugging down (whetting your whistle with) a nice cold beer or two.

❏ やっぱり男の人は、ぐいぐい引っ張ってくれるような人が頼もしくていいわ。

Yappari otoko no hito wa, guigui hippatte kureru yō na hito ga tanomoshikute ii wa.

After all is said and done, give me a strong man who takes the lead.

うつらうつら (utsura-utsura) N

To doze off. To drift back and forth between light sleep and drowsy wakefulness.

❏ 陽当たりのいい席だと、つい午後の授業はうつらうつらしてしまうんです。

Hiatari no ii seki da to, tsui gogo no jugyō wa utsura-utsura shite shimau n' desu.

If I get a seat in the sun during an afternoon class, I wind up nodding off.

❏ 目覚まし時計のベルを止めてから、ほんのちょっとうつらうつらするのが気持ちいいよね。

Mezamashi-dokei no beru o tomete kara, hon no chotto utsura-utsura suru no ga kimochi ii yo ne.

Switching off the alarm clock and then dozing off for a few more winks just can't be beat.

たっぷり (tappuri) G / N

Full, complete, more than sufficient, replete. Often used after a noun, as in 皮肉たっぷり *hiniku-tappuri* "awfully sarcastic," and 愛嬌たっぷり *aikyō-tappuri* "loaded with charm." When used before or after a numerical quantity, *tappuri* indicates that the quantity is met fully or even exceeded, as shown by the dialogue for this chapter.

❏ さっき*の課長の発言、いやみたっぷりだったと思いませんか。

Sakki no kachō no hatsugen, iyami tappuri datta to omoimasen ka.

Didn't you think that what the section chief said a while ago was just dripping with sarcasm?

❀ *Sakki*: colloquial version of *saki* (previous, earlier).

❑ 上着はむしろたっぷりしたものを選んだ方がきれいに着こ
なせます。

Uwagi wa mushiro tappuri shita mono o eranda hō ga kirei ni kikonase-masu.

I think you would look much better if you chose a looser fitting jacket.

うとうと (utouto) N

To fall into a light sleep. Used when one has fallen asleep without realizing it because of sickness or exhaustion.

❑ こたつに入ってテレビを見ているうちに、ついうとうととし
ちゃったわ。

Kotatsu ni haitte terebi o mite iru uchi ni, tsui utouto shichatta wa.

I was sitting in the *kotatsu* and watching TV, when before I knew it I had nodded off to sleep.

❑ いい気持ちでうとうととしていたのに、電話がかかってきて
たたき起こされちゃった＊よ。

Ii kimochi de utouto shite ita no ni, denwa ga kakatte kite tatakiokosarechatta yo.

I was just floating off into dreamland when the goddamn telephone rang and woke me up.

　＊ *Tatakiokosu*: rouse, roust, wake up.

➡ The *kotatsu* is a traditional Japanese heating device. In its original form, a small charcoal brazier is placed inside a square hole cut into the tatami or floor, and a small frame covered with a futon is put over the hole. To get warm, you stick your legs into the hole and wrap the edge of the futon around yourself. This is called a *horigotatsu*. These days, most *kotatsu* look like low, square tables that are placed directly on the tatami or carpet. An electric heater under the tabletop provides the warmth. While *horigotatsu* are more comfortable since you can let your legs dangle down, electric *kotatsu* are more convenient because you don't have to light the coals and there's no danger of carbon monoxide poisoning. For many Japanese, the ultimate in family togetherness during the winter is to sit snug and warm in the *kotatsu* while eating *mikan* (mandarin oranges).

うっかり (ukkari) B

To forget, miss, or fail to pay attention to something important.

❑ うっかりしてたなあ。きょう彼女と約束してたんだ。

Ukkari shite 'ta nā. Kyō kanojo to yakusoku shite 'ta n' da.

Darn it! I had a date with my girlfriend today and it completely slipped my mind.

❑ ごめんなさいね、酔っ払ってついうっかり口をすべらせちゃったのよ。

Gomen nasai ne, yopparatte tsui ukkari kuchi o suberasechatta no yo.

I'm really sorry. The liquor went to my head and it just slipped out.

Q u i z

A BIG HEADACHE

Fill in the blanks with one of the words studied in this chapter: むかむか mukamuka, くらくら kurakura, くどくど kudokudo, げんなり gennari, べろべろ berobero, ばりばり baribari, ぐいぐい guigui, うつらうつら utsurautsura, たっぷり tappuri, うとうと utouto, うっかり ukkari. There are at least two sentences for each word. Answers are on page 218.

１ あの場面は思い出しただけで（　　　　　）吐き気がするね。

Ano bamen wa omoidashita dake de (　　　　　) hakike ga suru ne.

Just thinking back about that sight makes me want to barf.

２ 高いところは苦手なのよ。高層ビルなんて上るだけで（　　　　　）しちゃうわ。

Takai tokoro wa nigate na no yo. Kōsōbiru nante agaru dake de (　　　　) shichau wa.

I simply hate high places. Just going up one of those tall buildings is enough to make my head spin.

３ （　　　　　）と説明してくれるんだけど、さっぱりわからないんだ。

(　　　　) to setsumei shite kureru n' da kedo, sappari wakaranai n' da.

He keeps explaining over and over, but I still don't have a clue what he's talking about.

4 いくら好_すきなものでも、毎食_{まいしょく}出_だされると（　　　　　）するよね。

Ikura suki na mono de mo, maishoku dasareru to (　　　　) suru yo ne.

No matter how much you like something, you get a little tired of having it for every meal.

5 うちの犬_{いぬ}、この餌_{えさ}が好_すきで、お皿_{さら}まで（　　　　　）なめまわしているのよ。

Uchi no inu, kono esa ga suki de, osara made (　　　　　) namemawashite iru no yo.

Our dog likes this food so much he licks the plate clean.

6 若_{わか}くて（　　　　　）働_{はたら}いている人_{ひと}を見_みると、うらやましいね。

Wakakute (　　　　) hataraite iru hito o miru to, urayamashii ne.

It makes me envious to see someone who's young and is working like a bull.

7 この間_{あいだ}のマラソンでは、最後_{さいご}の1キロで（　　　　）と引_ひき離_{はな}して勝_かったのよ。

Kono aida no marason de wa, saigo no ichi-kiro de (　　　) to hiki-hanashite katta no yo.

In the marathon the other day, I pulled away from the pack in the last kilometer and won.

8 暇_{ひま}さえあれば（　　　　）しているから、よっぽど疲_{つか}れているんだね。

Hima sae areba (　　　　) shite iru kara, yoppodo tsukarete iru n' da ne.

Whenever she has a spare moment, she dozes off. She must be really tired.

9 あの発言_{はつげん}は皮肉_{ひにく}（　　　　）だったね。

Ano hatsugen wa hiniku (   ) datta ne.

That comment was loaded with sarcasm, wasn't it.

10 (   )しかけた頃に、すごい音がするから、目が覚め
ちゃった。

(   ) *shikaketa koro ni, sugoi oto ga suru kara, me ga samechatta.*

Just as I was dropping off to sleep, there was this tremendous sound
that woke me up.

11 (   )していて、電車の中に傘を忘れてきちゃった。

(   ) *shite ite, densha no naka ni kasa o wasurete kichatta.*

My mind was somewhere else, and I forgot my umbrella in the
train.

12 きょうは二日酔いで胃が (   ) するんだ。

Kyō wa futsukayoi de i ga (   ) suru n' da.

I've got a hangover today and feel kind of queasy.

13 急に立ち上がったら、(   )めまいがしちゃったの。

Kyū ni tachiagattara, (   ) memai ga shichatta no.

When I stood up suddenly, I had a dizzy spell.

14 (   )言い訳ばかり言っていると信用をなくすよ。

(   ) *iiwake bakari itte iru to shinyō o nakusu yo.*

If all you do is make long, drawn-out excuses, no one's going to
trust you.

15 こう毎日電車事故が続くと、(   )するね。

Kō mainichi densha-jiko ga tsuzuku to, (   ) suru ne.

With a train accident every day of the week, it kind of gets you
down.

16 (　　　　　　　)になるまで飲むなんて、健康に悪いよ。

(　　　　　　) ni naru made nomu nante, kenkō ni warui yo.

Drinking until you're out of your head is not good for your health.

17 のりをつけすぎて、シーツが(　　　　　　)になっちゃった。

Nori o tsukesugite, shītsu ga (　　　　　) ni natchatta.

I used so much starch that the sheets got as stiff as boards.

18 日本酒をそんなに(　　　　　)飲んだら酔っ払いますよ。

Nihon-shu o sonna ni (　　　　　) nondara yopparaimasu yo.

If you keep tossing down sake like that, you'll end up drunk.

19 電車の中でつい(　　　　　)居眠りして、乗り過ごしたんだ。

Densha no naka de tsui (　　　　　) inemuri shite, norisugoshita n' da.

In the train I kept dozing off and missed my stop.

20 時間は(　　　　　)あるから、慌てなくていいですよ。

Jikan wa (　　　　　) aru kara, awatenakute ii desu yo.

We have plenty of time. No need to worry about that.

21 テレビをつけっぱなしで、つい(　　　　　)しちゃったんだ。

Terebi o tsukeppanashi de, tsui (　　　　　) shichatta n' da.

With the TV going full blast, I ended up dropping off to sleep.

22 (　　　　　　)お財布を持ってくるのを忘れちゃった。

(　　　　　　) osaifu o motte kuru no o wasurechatta.

I don't know what I was thinking, but I completely forgot to bring my wallet.

FEELING OUT OF SORTS?

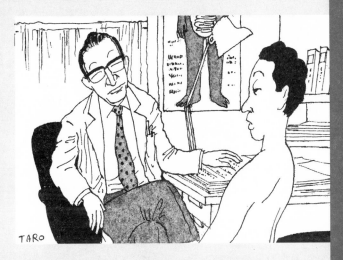

TARO

Masaru Kodera, who works at the Nippon Real Estate Co., is feeling out of sorts, so he's gone to a clinic for a checkup. Dr. Akio Kadota, a specialist in internal medicine, is now examining him.

門田　　「どうしました？」

小寺　　「どうも風邪をこじらせたみたいで。最初はのどが**ひりひ
　　　　り**する程度だったんですけど、そのうちせきも出るように
　　　　なって、夜中にのどが**ぜいぜい**するんです。」

門田　　「どんなせきが出ますか。**こんこん**とか、**ごほんごほん**と
　　　　か……。」

小寺　　「**ごほんごほん**という感じですね。」

門田　　「熱はありますか。」

小寺　　「はい、きのうから。夕べは**ぞくぞく**寒気がしたので、高
　　　　熱が出るんじゃないかと**ひやひや**したんですが、今のとこ
　　　　ろ*7度8分くらいでおさまっています。」

門田　　「食欲はどうですか。」

小寺　　「**もりもり**というわけにはいきませんが、まあまあありま
　　　　す。あと、目が**しょぼしょぼ**して頭も重いんです。」

門田　　「他には？」

小寺　　「胃が**しくしく**痛むことがあります。それと、あのう……。
　　　　実は、先生、どうしても会社に行きたくないんです。」

❀ *Ima no tokoro*: at present, for the moment.

Kadota:	*Dō shimashita?*
Kodera:	*Dōmo kaze o kojiraseta mitai de. Saisho wa nodo ga hirihiri suru teido datta n' desu kedo, sono uchi seki mo deru yō ni natte, yonaka ni nodo ga zeizei suru n' desu.*
Kadota:	*Donna seki ga demasu ka. Konkon to ka, gohongohon to ka...*
Kodera:	*Gohongohon to iu kanji desu ne.*
Kadota:	*Netsu wa arimasu ka.*
Kodera:	*Hai, kinō kara. Yūbe wa zokuzoku samuke ga shita no de, kōnetsu ga deru n' ja nai ka to hiyahiya shita n' desu ga, ima no tokoro nana-do hachi-bu kurai de osamatte imasu.*
Kadota:	*Shokuyoku wa dō desu ka.*
Kodera:	*Morimori to iu wake ni wa ikimasen ga, māmā arimasu. Ato, me ga shoboshobo shite atama mo omoi n' desu.*
Kadota:	*Hoka ni wa?*
Kodera:	*I ga shikushiku itamu koto ga arimasu. Sore to, anō... Jitsu wa, sensei, dōshite mo kaisha ni ikitaku nai n' desu.*

✳ ✳ ✳

Kadota:	So what's the problem?
Kodera:	I think I've aggravated a cold. At first my throat was just a little prickly, but then I started coughing. Late at night I get all wheezy.
Kadota:	What kind of cough is it? Just a regular cough, or are you really hacking?
Kodera:	More like hacking.
Kadota:	Do you have a fever?

Kodera: Yes, I do, since yesterday. Last night I came down with the chills and started shivering, and I was afraid I'd get a really high fever. Now it's only about 37.8°C [100°F], though.

Kadota: Do you have much of an appetite?

Kodera: I'm not exactly shoveling it down, but I'm eating all right. Other than that, my eyes are sort of watery, and my head feels like a ton of bricks.

Kadota: Anything else?

Kodera: Sometimes I get this dull pain in my stomach, and, um, uh … To tell you the truth, Doc, I just don't feel like going to work.

ひりひり (hirihiri) N / B

A feeling of continuous pain or irritation on the skin, inside the mouth or nose, etc.

❑ どうも背中がひりひりすると思ったら、日焼けで水ぶくれができていたんです。

Dōmo senaka ga hirihiri suru to omottara, hiyake de mizubukure ga dekite ita n' desu.

I had this funny stinging feeling on my back, and what should it be but blisters from my sunburn.

❑ タイ料理はうまいですね。ひりひりする辛さが、こたえられません*よ。

Tai-ryōri wa umai desu ne. Hirihiri suru karasa ga, kotaeraremasen yo.

Thai food sure is good. I love the tingling feeling the spices give you.

> ❈ *Kotaeru:* to bear, endure; in the negative, can't bear something (because it is so good).

ぜいぜい (zeizei) N / B

The sound or feeling of air being forced through the windpipe due to a cold or other respiratory illness.

❏ そんなにぜいぜいしているん␣なら、医者に診てもらった方がいいんじゃないですか。

Sonna ni zeizei shite iru n' nara, isha ni mite moratta hō ga ii n' ja nai desu ka.

With a wheeze like that, don't you think you should have a doctor take a look at you?

❏ ぜん息は怖いですよ。発作が起こるとぜいぜいして死ぬかと思いますよ。

Zensoku wa kowai desu yo. Hossa ga okoru to zeizei shite shinu ka to omoimasu yo.

Asthma is really scary. When I get an attack, I feel like I'm going to wheeze myself to death.

こんこん (konkon) N / B

A light cough. Small children use this word to describe coughing in general.

❏ 明け方になるとこんこんせきが出て、目が覚めるんです。

Akegata ni naru to konkon seki ga dete, me ga sameru n' desu.

Around dawn I start coughing and it wakes me up.

❏ こんこんが出るから、暖かくして早く寝なさい。

Konkon ga deru kara, atatakaku shite hayaku nenasai.

You'll get a cough, so make yourself warm and go right to bed. (Said to a child.)

ごほんごほん (gohongohon) N / B

The sound of a loud, heavy cough from deep in the throat or any wet, phlegmy cough.

❏ 人の顔に向かってごほんごほんとせきをするなんて、失礼ね。

Hito no kao ni mukatte gohongohon to seki o suru nante, shitsurei ne.

It's so rude to let loose with a hacking cough right in someone's face like that.

❏ 課長ったら、ごほんごほんとせき込みながらもタバコを離さないのよ。どうか*と思うわ。

Kachō ttara, gohongohon to sekikominagara mo tabako o hanasanai no yo. Dōka to omou wa.

The section chief is really something. He keeps on smoking even when he's coughing his head off. I can't believe it!

❋ *Dōka*: expresses wonder or perplexity at some uncommon situation.

ぞくぞく (zokuzoku) G / N / B

Shivering with cold (N/B) or with pleasure, expectation, nervousness, fear, etc. (G/N/B).

❏ 何だか*背すじがぞくぞくするんです。熱が上がりそうなので早退させてください。

Nan da ka sesuji ga zokuzoku suru n' desu. Netsu ga agarisō na no de sōtai sasete kudasai.

I'm getting chills up and down my back, and I think my temperature is going up. Is it all right if I leave early?

❋ *Nan da ka*: for some reason or other.

❑ このミステリーはおもしろいよ。ぞくぞくするほどスリリングなんだ。

Kono misuterī wa omoshiroi yo. Zokuzoku suru hodo suriringu nan da.

This mystery is really great. It's so thrilling it gives me the chills.

ひやひや (hiyahiya) B

The feeling of fear or worry in a dangerous situation. Originally a cold or chilly feeling.

❑ やっぱりうそなんかつくもんじゃないなあ。いつばれる*
かとひやひやしたよ。

Yappari uso nanka tsuku mon ja nai nā. Itsu bareru ka to hiyahiya shita yo.

Lying just isn't worth it, after all. I was scared stiff that I'd get caught any minute.

　　※ *Bareru*: to come into the open.

❑ 彼の車に乗るのはひやひやものよ。飲むわとばす*わで、命がいくつあっても足りない†わ。

Kare no kuruma ni noru no wa hiyahiya-mono yo. Nomu wa tobasu wa de, inochi ga ikutsu atte mo tarinai wa.

Riding with him is enough to make your hair curl. The way he drinks and burns up the road, it gives you the feeling you're living on borrowed time.

　　※ *… wa … wa*: doing both one thing and the other.

　　† *Inochi ga ikutsu atte mo tarinai*: lit., "no matter how many lives one had, they wouldn't be enough."

もりもり (morimori) G

To be full, strong, powerful. By extension, to be very hungry, eager, peppy. The word also describes an action that is performed vigorously, enthusiastically, energetically.

❑ 堀田さんはボディビルをやっているだけあって、筋肉もりもりだよ。

Hotta-san wa bodībiru o yatte iru dake atte, kinniku morimori da yo.

The way Hotta has been hitting the weights, it's no wonder his muscles are practically popping (bulging) out of his skin.

❑ もりもり食べるだけじゃなくて、もりもり働いてほしいもんだね。

Morimori taberu dake ja nakute, morimori hataraite hoshii mon da ne.

I wish he wouldn't just eat like a horse but would work like one, too.

しょぼしょぼ (shoboshobo) B

(1) To have bleary, sleepy, or squinty eyes. (2) A continuous gloomy drizzle; getting wet and feeling miserable in such weather. (3) A listless, lackluster feeling.

❑ 夕べ日本語の擬音語・擬態語についての本を読み出したらやめられなくなってね、おかげで*今日は目がしょぼしょぼだよ。

Yūbe Nihon-go no gion-go–gitai-go ni tsuite no hon o yomidashitara yamerarenaku natte ne, okage de kyō wa me ga shoboshobo da yo.

Last night I started reading a book on Japanese onomotopoeia and mimesis, and I just couldn't put it down. That's why my eyes are all puffy today.

❋ *Okage de*: thanks to (that).

□ 雨がしょぼしょぼ降っていると、どうも買い物に出るのが
　おっくうになるわね。

*Ame ga shoboshobo futte iru to, dōmo kaimono ni deru no ga okkū ni
naru wa ne.*

When it's drizzly out, it's too much of a bother to go out shopping,
isn't it.

□ やっぱり年かなあ、おやじの後ろ姿が何とも*しょぼしょ
　ぼしているんだよ。

*Yappari toshi ka nā, oyaji no ushirosugata ga nan to mo shoboshobo shite
iru n' da yo.*

Dad's getting on, I guess. Seen from behind, he just seems to be
doddering along.

　❋ *Nan to mo*: inexpressably.

しくしく (shikushiku) N / B

(1) A pain that is sharp and continuous but not too strong (B). (2)
Prolonged sniveling, whimpering, sniffling (N).

□ 虫歯*がしくしく痛んで夕べは眠れませんでした。

Mushiba ga shikushiku itande yūbe wa nemuremasen deshita.

I couldn't sleep last night because this toothache just wouldn't let up.

　❋ *Mushiba*: cavity, dental caries.

□ 道端でしくしく泣いている女の子がいるから誰かと思った
　ら、美雪ちゃんじゃないの。

*Michibata de shikushiku naite iru onna no ko ga iru kara dare ka to
omottara, Miyuki-chan ja nai no.*

I was wondering who the little girl sniffling beside the road was, and
who should it be but little Miyuki!

➥ Unless you're speaking to a very close friend or relative, you need to tack a suffix onto the name of the person you're talking to. The choice of a suffix reflects the formality of the occasion, the psychological distance between you and the other person, and where you stand relative to him or her in the social hierarchy.

-*San* ～ さん is the most common, of course. It is found in all kinds of situations, uttered by both men and women, young and old. For very formal occasions or when being very polite to a social superior, you might opt for ～様 -*sama*, but be sure to accompany it with the proper honorific, humble, and polite forms, or whatever you can muster in that regard. In day-to-day life, you're most likely to hear -*sama* used by tellers in banks or clerks in department stores to address their customers.

When you're speaking to a close friend or colleague who's at the same or a lower level in rank, you might want to use ～ちゃん -*chan* or ～くん -*kun* (also written 君) after the first (especially with -*chan*) or the last name, the former most often in reference to women, the latter to men. When -*chan* is used after the full last name, however, it can leave an impression of coarseness. The level of speech should reflect the implied intimacy. (-*Chan* is also the most common suffix for talking to or about babies and children, especially girls; -*kun* is frequently used for boys.)

When two Japanese speakers meet each other for the first time, they have to size each other up to determine what kind of language to use. The important factors include age, social group, job, rank, and accomplishments, and a mistake can be embarrassing. This helps to explain the popularity of business cards: they let people pigeonhole each other at a glance.

Quiz

Feeling Out of Sorts?

Fill in the blanks with one of the words studied in this chapter: ひりひり hirihiri, ぜいぜい zeizei, こんこん konkon, ごほんごほん gohongohon, ぞくぞく zokuzoku, ひやひや hiyahiya, もりもり morimori, しょぼしょぼ shoboshobo, しくしく shikushiku. There are at least two sentences for each word. Answers are on page 218.

1 空気が乾燥しているんだね。鼻の中が（　　　　　）するよ。

Kūki ga kansō shite iru n' da ne. Hana no naka ga (　　　　) suru yo.

The air is really dry, isn't it. I have this prickly feeling inside my nose.

2 風邪は治ったはずなのに、ちょっと走ると（　　　　　）してしまうんだ。

Kaze wa naotta hazu na no ni, chotto hashiru to (　　　　) shite shimau n' da.

I thought I was over my cold, but whenever I run a little I end up wheezing.

3 （　　　　　）という軽いせきでも、続くようだったら検査をしたほうがいいですね。

(　　　　) to iu karui seki de mo, tsuzuku yō dattara kensa o shita hō ga ii desu ne.

Even if it's a slight cough, you should have it checked if it continues.

4 今の風邪は（　　　　　）と痰のからんだようなせきが出るらしいよ。

Ima no kaze wa (　　　　　) to tan no karanda yō na seki ga deru rashii yo.

The cold that's going around produces a heavy cough with phlegm.

5 （　　　　　）するくらい怖い話だね。

(　　　　　) suru kurai kowai hanashi da ne.

That story is enough to give you goose bumps.

6 切り立った崖のところをバスが通るから、乗っていても（　　　　　）したわ。

Kiritatta gake no tokoro o basu ga tōru kara, notte ite mo (　　　　　) shita wa.

The bus was traveling along this steep cliff, and inside, I got this clammy feeling all over.

7 負けず嫌いだから、やる気が（　　　　　）わいてきた。

Makezu-girai da kara, yaru ki ga (　　　　　) waite kita.

I hate to lose, so I'm raring to go.

8 雨が（　　　　　）降っていてうっとうしいね。

Ame ga (　　　　　) futte ite uttōshii ne.

Drizzling all the time, it's really depressing.

9 あの子、お母さんがいない間ずっと（　　　　　）泣いていたよ。

Ano ko, okāsan ga inai aida zutto (　　　　　) naite ita yo.

The child was whimpering the whole time his mother was gone.

10 転んですりむいたところが（　　　　　）するんだ。

Koronde surimuita tokoro ga (　　　　　) suru n' da.

I have this prickly feeling where I fell and scraped my skin.

11 のどが（　　　　　）するので医者に行って来るよ。

Nodo ga (　　　　　) suru no de isha ni itte kuru yo.

My throat is making a wheezing sound, so I'm going to see a doctor.

12 （　　　　　）がでるから、お風呂に入るのはやめようね。（子供に）

（　　　　　） *ga deru kara, ofuro ni hairu no wa yameyō ne.*

Let's not take a bath, okay, because you'll get a cough. (Spoken to a small child.)

13 こんこんというせきから（　　　　　）という重いせきに変わったんです。

Konkon to iu seki kara (　　　　　) to iu omoi seki ni kawatta n' desu.

It changed from a slight cough to a heavy one.

14 どうも朝から（　　　　　）すると思ったら、熱が出ちゃった。

Dōmo asa kara (　　　　　) suru to omottara, netsu ga dechatta.

From morning on I had the chills, and, just as I thought, I came down with a temperature.

15 渋滞に巻き込まれて、時間に間に合うかどうか（　　　　　）したよ。

Jūtai ni makikomarete, jikan ni ma ni au ka dō ka (　　　　　) shita yo.

Caught in traffic, I broke out in a cold sweat wondering whether we would make it in time.

16 ああ、腹が減った。（　　　　　）食べるぞ。

Aa, hara ga hetta. (　　　　　) taberu zo.

Boy, am I starved. I think I'll just eat everything on the table.

Q u i z

Feeling Out of Sorts?　119

17 パソコンって、目が疲れるね。もう（　　　　）だよ。

Pasokon tte, me ga tsukareru ne. Mō (　　　　) da yo.

PCs are awfully hard on the eyes. Mine are all bleary.

18 昨日から歯が（　　　　）痛むの。

Kinō kara ha ga (　　　　) itamu no.

I've had this nagging toothache since yesterday.

THE TRIALS OF MIDDLE MANAGERS

Yoshihide Kakinuma and Yūji Seki are managers at Sakura Publishing Company. Here they are having lunch together in the company cafeteria.

柿沼 「最近の新入社員には**やきもき**させられますよ。」

関 「同感ですね。」

柿沼 「**やんわり**指示すると何にもしない。かといって*、**ばしっ
と**言うと**ぷうっと**ふくれる。」

関 「やはり子供の少ない時代で甘やかされて育ったからで
しょうか。手取り足取り†言わないと、ただ**ぼけっと**してい
る、といった感じですね。」

柿沼 「かと思うと*、ふだん**ぼそぼそ**しゃべるくせに、カラオケ
に行くと人が変わったようにマイクを離さなかったりし
て。」

関 「どういうんでしょうね。この間も、あんまり**ぐずぐず**して
いるんで急がせたら、**ぶすっと**したかと思うと、目に涙を
ためているんですよ。」

柿沼 「**めそめそ**されるとこっちも困るし、言い方が難しいです
ね。」

関 「全くです。会社でめそめそ、家で**ぎゃあぎゃあ**…泣きた
いのはこっちの方ですよ。」

❖ *Ka to itte*: used to introduce a contrary or additional comment; similar to "having
said that."

† *Tetori-ashitori*: lit., "taking hand, taking foot"; to take someone by the hand and show
how to do something.

❖ *Ka to omou to*: indicating successive actions (e.g., "and at the same time"), in this
case the preceding and succeeding sentences.

Kakinuma:	*Saikin no shinnyū-shain ni wa yakimoki saseraremasu yo.*
Seki:	*Dōkan desu ne.*
Kakinuma:	*Yanwari shiji suru to nanni mo shinai. Ka to itte, bashitto iu to pūtto fukureru.*
Seki:	*Yahari kodomo no sukunai jidai de amayakasarete sodatta kara deshō ka. Tetori-ashitori iwanai to, tada boketto shite iru, to itta kanji desu ne.*
Kakinuma:	*Ka to omou to, fudan bosoboso shaberu kuse ni, karaoke ni iku to hito ga kawatta yō ni maiku o hanasanakattari shite.*
Seki:	*Dō iu n' deshō ne. Kono aida mo, anmari guzuguzu shite iru n' de isogasetara, busutto shita ka to omou to, me ni namida o tamete iru n' desu yo.*
Kakinuma:	*Mesomeso sareru to kotchi mo komaru shi, iikata ga muzukashii desu ne.*
Seki:	*Mattaku desu. Kaisha de mesomeso, ie de gyāgyā... Nakitai no wa kotchi no hō desu yo.*

✼ ✼ ✼

Kakinuma:	The new employees these days really keep you guessing.
Seki:	I feel the same way.
Kakinuma:	If I tell them to do something nicely, they don't do anything at all. Then if I lay down the law, they start pouting.
Seki:	What with smaller families these days, maybe they're all growing up spoiled. If you don't spell everything out, they just sit there with their eyes glazed over.
Kakinuma:	On the other hand, while they just mumble under their breath most of the time, their whole personality changes when they go to karaoke. Then they won't let go of the mike.

Seki: How can you explain it? The other day one of them was taking her own sweet time with her work, so I hurried her up a bit. No sooner had she gotten all bent out of shape than her eyes filled up with tears.

Kakinuma: I hate it when they start whining. It's hard to know what to say.

Seki: You're absolutely right. With the employees whining at us at the office and the wife and kids raising a ruckus at home, we're the ones who should be crying.

やきもき (yakimoki) B

To fret, fuss, worry, feel anxious.

❏ いくら回りがやきもきしても、本人がやる気を起こさなけれ
ば大学には合格しないよ。

Ikura mawari ga yakimoki shite mo, honnin ga yaru ki o okosanakereba daigaku ni wa gōkaku shinai yo.

It doesn't matter how much the people around him bite their nails. If he doesn't get his act together, he'll never get into college.

❏ ひどい渋滞に巻きこまれちゃって、結婚式に間に合わないん
じゃないかとやきもきしたわ。

Hidoi jūtai ni makikomarechatte, kekkon-shiki ni ma ni awanai n' ja nai ka to yakimoki shita wa.

We got stuck in a terrible traffic jam. I was afraid we'd be late for the wedding.

やんわり (yanwari) N

Softly, gently. Describes polite or indirect expressions that are used to soften criticisms, reprimands, etc.

❑ 社会に出たら、相手のいやみをやんわり受け流せるくらいの
　ゆとりはほしいね。

Shakai ni detara, aite no iyami o yanwari ukenagaseru kurai no yutori wa hoshii ne.

Once you get out of school and start working in the real world, you should be flexible (big-minded) enough to shrug off the mean little things people say.

❑ そんなことでどなりつけなくて゜も、やんわりと言って聞かせ
　ればわかるんですよ。

Sonna koto de donaritsukenakute mo, yanwari to itte kikasereba wakaru n' desu yo.

There's no need to yell like that. Just speak softly and he'll get the point.

　　※ *Donaritsukeru*: to yell at, scream at.

ばしっと (bashitto) N

(1) The cracking sound of dry wood or another hard, thick object splitting, breaking, or hitting something. (2) Actions or words that are firm, unyielding, decisive, adamant.

❑ 打った瞬間ばしっと音がしたと思ったら゜、ラケットが折れ
　ちゃってね、カッコわるかったよ。

Utta shunkan bashitto oto ga shita to omottara, raketto ga orechatte ne, kakko warukatta yo.

I heard a cracking sound the instant I hit the ball—my racket had broken in two. Boy, did I look stupid.

　　※ *To omottara*: almost as soon as something comes to awareness, another event occurs; when, as soon as, at the moment of.

❏ あんまりしつこく誘われるから、ばしっと断わっちゃったわ。

Anmari shitsukoku sasowareru kara, bashitto kotowatchatta wa.

He made such a nuisance of himself asking me out that I finally turned him down flat.

ぷうっと (pūtto) N / B

(1) A sudden blast or honk from a horn, trumpet, etc., or a snorting sound emitted from the mouth or another bodily orifice. Also used to describe unsuccessfully suppressed laughter (N). (2) An object being inflated quickly (N). (3) A pouty expression of discontent— lower lip distended, cheeks puffed out, etc. (B).

❏ この辺は、夕方になるとぷうっとラッパをふきながらお豆腐屋さんが回ってくるのよ。

Kono hen wa, yūgata ni naru to pūtto rappa o fukinagara otōfuya-san ga mawatte kuru no yo.

Every evening, a tofu seller comes by here tooting on a horn.

❏ あまりのおかしさに、思わずぷうっと吹き出しちゃった。

Amari no okashisa ni, omowazu pūtto fukidashichatta.

It was so funny I couldn't help but burst out laughing.

❏ このおもち、そろそろ食べ頃よ。焼けてぷうっとふくれてきたもの。

Kono omochi, sorosoro tabegoro yo. Yakete pūtto fukurete kita mono.

It's about time to eat this *mochi*. It's all big and puffy now.

❏ 気に入らないとすぐぷうっとふくれるんじゃ、まるで*子供と同じじゃないか。

Ki ni iranai to sugu pūtto fukureru n' ja, maru de kodomo to onaji ja nai ka.

You're just like a little kid, the way you start pouting (get grumpy) whenever you don't like something.

❀ *Maru de*: exactly like.

➥ *Mochi* is a kind of thick, sticky paste made from a special kind of rice that has been steamed, kneaded, and shaped into a round or square cake. Eaten either raw or cooked, it is often a special treat at New Year's and during celebrations. Cooked, it swells slightly.

ぼけっと (boketto) N / B

To gaze vacantly off into space, without thinking or doing anything (N/B). Used critically of someone who sits around and doesn't notice work that needs to be done (B).

❏ たまには海でも見ながら、一日中ぼけっとして過ごしたいなあ。

Tama ni wa umi de mo minagara, ichinichi-jū boketto shite sugoshitai nā.

Sometimes I just want to spend the whole day taking it easy, gazing at the ocean or something.

❏ 何をぼけっとそんなところで突っ立ってるんだ、危ないじゃないか。

Nani o boketto sonna tokoro de tsuttatte 'ru n' da, abunai ja nai ka.

What are you doing standing there like a goddamn telephone pole? Don't you know it's dangerous?

ぼそぼそ (bosoboso) B

(1) Spoken in a hushed, unclear voice. (2) Of food: dry, tasteless, unappetizing.

❏ あの人、いつもぼそぼそと話して何となく陰気な感じね。

Ano hito, itsumo bosoboso to hanashite nan to naku inki na kanji ne.

There's something spooky about that fellow, the way he talks under his breath all the time.

❏ ご飯に麦を混ぜると、体にはいいかもしれないけど、何だか ぼそぼそするわね。

Gohan ni mugi o mazeru to, karada ni wa ii kamo shirenai kedo, nan da ka bosoboso suru wa ne.

Rice mixed with barley might be good for your health, but somehow it tastes like sawdust.

➡ Rice is the staple food of Japan, of course, particularly white rice that is boiled and served without any flavoring. Starchy, sticky rice is especially prized, with varieties like *sasanishiki* and *koshihikari* fetching high prices for their agglutinating texture.

ぐずぐず (guzuguzu) B

(1) To stretch out a job, vacillate, procrastinate, waste time. (2) Used to describe a whiny, fussy, demanding child or a grumbling, complaining adult who acts like a child. (3) Of clothing etc.: loose, baggy, unshapen. (4) The sound or feeling of a stuffy nose.

❏ ぐずぐずしていると学校に遅れますよ。

Guzuguzu shite iru to gakkō ni okuremasu yo.

If you keep dawdling (fooling around), you're going to be late for school.

❏ 何をぐずぐずしているんだ。さっさととりかかりなさい。

Nani o guzuguzu shite iru n' da. Sassa to torikakarinasai.

What are you dragging your feet for? Get cracking!

❏ 子供じゃあるまいし*、いつまでぐずぐず言っているんだ。

Kodomo ja aru mai shi, itsu made guzuguzu itte iru n' da.

You aren't a young kid, for God's sake. How long are you going to
keep fussing? (Grow up and stop whining like a baby!)

> ❊ *Ja aru mai shi*: in spite of the fact that you are not *something*, with strong
> critical overtones.

❏ 着付けがうまくないもんだから、帯がぐずぐずにゆるん
じゃったわ。

*Kitsuke ga umaku nai mon da kara, obi ga guzuguzu ni yurunjatta
wa.*

My *obi* wasn't tied properly, so now it's coming loose.

❏ 毎年この季節になると、花粉症で鼻がぐずぐずするわ、頭は
重いわで憂うつなんですよ。

*Mai-nen kono kisetsu ni naru to, kafun-shō de hana ga guzuguzu suru
wa, atama wa omoi wa de yūutsu nan desu yo.*

Every year about this time, I get the sniffles from hay fever, and my
heads get all clogged up—boy, is it depressing.

➡ *Kitsuke* refers to the way a kimono is put on. It takes skill and experience to
adjust the *obi*, cords, and folds so that a kimono fits well. In the past, most Japanese
women could do it themselves, but that skill has been lost as dresses, skirts, blouses,
and slacks have become the common wear for day-to-day life. These days, if a
woman wants to wear a kimono to, say, a wedding ceremony, she probably goes to a
beauty parlor to be dressed by a professional fitter.

ぶすっと (busutto) N / B

(1) The sound or feeling of a thick, soft material being pierced by a sharp, hard object (N). (2) Used to describe sullen anger or discontent (B).

❏ 氷を割っていて、アイスピックでぶすっと指を刺しちゃったのよ。痛かったわ。

Kōri o watte ite, aisupikku de busutto yubi o sashichatta no yo. Itakatta wa.

When I was breaking the ice, I jabbed my finger with the ice pick. It really hurt.

❏ あのお店の人はいつもぶすっとしていて愛想*がないわね。

Ano omise no hito wa itsumo busutto shite ite aisō ga nai wa ne.

The clerks at that store aren't very friendly. They always seem to be sulking.

    ❀ *Aiso*: amiability, sociability, hospitality.

めそめそ (mesomeso) B

Whimpering, whining, sniveling. Often used to describe a timorous person who breaks into tears over trifles.

❏ 失恋*ぐらいでいつまでもめそめそするなよ。

Shitsuren gurai de itsu made mo mesomeso suru na yo.

Just because you have a broken heart, don't keep moaning and groaning about it forever.

    ❀ *Shitsuren*: disappointed or unrequited love.

❏ めそめそ泣いてばかりいないで、たまには気分転換*でもしたらどうだ。

Mesomeso naite bakari inai de, tama ni wa kibun-tenkan de mo shi-tara dō da.

Don't just sit around whimpering like a baby! Do something different for a change.

❊ *Kibun-tenkan*: a change of mood.

ぎゃあぎゃあ (gyāgyā) B

(1) The sound of noisy crying or screeching by children, birds, animals, etc. With animals, the word can imply an unpleasant or eerie feeling. (2) Complaining, bitching, whining, griping.

❑ 隣の赤ん坊がぎゃあぎゃあ夜泣きするんで、このところ寝不足だよ。

Tonari no akanbō ga gyāgyā yonaki suru n' de, kono tokoro nebusoku da yo.

The baby next door has been bawling at night, so I haven't gotten much sleep lately.

❑ 女房子供にぎゃあぎゃあせがまれて、連休にディズニーランドへ行ってきたんだ。

Nyōbō kodomo ni gyāgyā segamarete, renkyū ni Dizunīrando e itte kita n' da.

My wife and kids had been pestering me about it, so we went to Disneyland over the long weekend.

Quiz

Fill in the blanks with one of the words studied in this chapter: やきもき yakimoki, やんわり yanwari, ばしっと bashitto, ぷうっと pūtto, ぼけっと boketto, ぼそぼそ bosoboso, ぐずぐず guzuguzu, ぶすっと busutto, めそめそ mesomeso, ぎゃあぎゃあ gyāgyā. There are at least two sentences for each word. Answers are on page 219.

1 まわりがいくら（　　　　　　）と気をもんでも本人がその気にならないとだめだよ。

Mawari ga ikura (　　　　　) to ki o monde mo honnin ga sono ki ni naranai to dame da yo.

If he's not up to doing it himself, it doesn't matter how much other people fret and worry over it.

2 あの様子では、どうやら（　　　　　）効いてきたようね。

Ano yōsu de wa, dō yara (　　　　　) kiite kita yō da ne.

Judging from appearances, it seems to be slowly taking effect.

3 （　　　　　）スマッシュが決まって、ゲームが終わった。

(　　　　　) sumasshu ga kimatte, gēmu ga owatta.

With a final hard overhead smash the game came to an end.

4 ちょっと何か言われると（　　　　　）ふくれるんじゃ、まるで子供だね。

Chotto nani ka iwareru to (*) fukureru n' ja, marude kodomo da ne.*

If you get all bent out of shape every time someone says something to you, you're acting like a little kid.

5 (　　　　)立ってないで、ちょっと手伝ってよ。

(　　　　) tatte 'nai de, chotto tetsudatte yo.

Don't just stand there like a dumbbell. Give me a hand.

6 このお米は(　　　　)しているけど、ピラフにするとおいしいわよ。

Kono okome wa (　　　　) shite iru kedo, pirafu ni suru to oishii wa yo.

This rice is dry and crumbly, but it would make nice pilaf.

7 あの人、どうしていつも(　　　　)しているのかしら。

Ano hito, dōshite itsumo (　　　　) shite iru no kashira.

I can't understand why he always seems to be out of sorts.

8 いつまでも(　　　　)してたって仕方がないだろう。

Itsu made mo (　　　　) shite 'ta tte shikata ga nai darō.

It doesn't pay to be crying over spilt milk forever.

9 赤ん坊が(　　　　)泣いているけど、どうしたんだろう。

Akanbō ga (　　　　) naite iru kedo, dō shita n' darō.

What's happened to the baby? It's bawling its head off.

10 何を(　　　　)しているの？結婚は縁のものだよ。

Nani o (　　　　) shite iru no? Kekkon wa en no mono da yo.

What are you fretting about? Marriage is just a matter of luck.

11 (　　　　)注意したくらいじゃ、あの人には通じないよ。

(　　　　　) *chūi shita kurai ja, ano hito ni wa tsūjinai yo.*

If you just give him a gentle warning, he'll never get the point.

12 言うときは手加減せずに（　　　　　）言ってやったほうがいい
よ。

Iu toki wa tekagen sezu ni (　　　　) itte yatta hō ga ii yo.

When you do say something, don't hold back but lay it on the line.

13 風船を（　　　　　）ふくらませてごらん。

Fūsen o (　　　　) fukuramasete goran.

Try blowing into the balloon and making it big.

14 何を（　　　　　）しているの？お湯がわいているよ。

Nani o (　　　　) shite iru no? Oyu ga waite iru yo.

What are you standing there like a dummy for? The water's come to
a boil.

15 隣の部屋で（　　　　　）話しているのが聞こえるわね。

Tonari no heya de (　　　　) hanashite iru no ga kikoeru wa ne.

You can hear them mumbling things to each other in the next
room, can't you.

16 （　　　　　）してると、おいていくよ。

（　　　　　） *shite iru to, oite iku yo.*

If you don't get cracking, we'll leave you behind.

17 寒くなると鼻が（　　　　　）いうんだ。

Samuku naru to hana ga (　　　　) iu n' da.

As soon as it gets cold I get the sniffles.

18 調べたら、大きな釘がタイヤに（　　　　　）刺さっていた。

Shirabetara, ōkina kugi ga taiya ni (   ) sasatte ita.

When I took a look, this big nail was sticking out of the tire.

19 (）泣かれると気がめいるよ。

(   ) *nakareru to ki ga meiru yo.*

It really gets me when someone breaks down and cries like that.

20 (）わめけばいいというものでもないよ。

(   ) *wamekeba ii to iu mono de mo nai yo.*

If you think that making a big fuss will do the trick, you've got another think coming.

A SPAT

TARO

Mr. and Mrs. Ogawa are in their eighth year of marriage. They expected to have a good time playing tennis on Sunday afternoon, but...

由美 「昼間のあなたは何よ。恥ずかしいったらありゃしない＊。女の子に**じいっと**見とれちゃって。」

厚 「何を**ぷりぷり**してるのかと思ったらそんなことか。」

由美 「そんなことじゃありませんよ。みっともない。」

厚 「**ぴちぴち**した若い子に見とれてどこが悪いんだよ。」

由美 「思い出しても**ぞうっと**するわ。**にたにた**鼻の下を伸ばしちゃって†さ。」

厚 「おまえだってあやしいもんだよ。コーチと**いちゃいちゃ**してたじゃないか。」

由美 「そんなんじゃないわよ、失礼ね。あなたこそ何よ。ギャルが隣に来ただけで**そわそわ**しちゃって。いい年してばかみたい。」

厚 「ばかみたいで悪かった❖な。」

由美 「だいたい今時若い女の子に**ちやほや**してもらおうなんて甘いわよ。その**ぶよぶよ**のお腹。どこから見たって単なるおじさんのくせに❀。」

厚 「その単なるおじさんに**めろめろ**だったのはどこのどいつ✚だよ。」

❋ *Arya shinai*: emphatic negative (contraction of *ari wa shinai*) following *tara*.

† *Hana no shita o nobasu*: lit., "to stretch out the underside of the nose," i.e., the supposedly lascivious upper lip.

❖ *Warukatta*: roughly, "that was a disservice"; I'm sorry; excuse me (used here sarcastically).

❀ *Kuse ni*: in spite of the fact that (used derogatorily).

✚ *Doitsu*: who (derogatorily).

Yumi:	*Hiruma no anata wa nani yo. Hazukashii ttara arya shi-nai. Onna no ko ni jītto mitorechatte.*
Atsushi:	*Nani o puripuri shite 'ru no ka to omottara sonna koto ka.*
Yumi:	*Sonna koto ja arimasen yo. Mittomo-nai.*
Atsushi:	*Pichipichi shita wakai ko ni mitorete doko ga warui n' da yo.*
Yumi:	*Omoidashite mo zōtto suru wa. Nitanita hana no shita o nobashichatte sa.*
Atsushi:	*Omae datte ayashii mon da yo. Kōchi to ichaicha shite 'ta ja nai ka.*
Yumi:	*Sonna n' koto ja nai wa yo, shitsurei ne. Anata koso nani yo. Gyaru ga tonari ni kita dake de sowasowa shichatte. Ii toshi shite baka mitai.*
Atsushi:	*Baka mitai de warukatta na.*
Yumi:	*Daitai ima-doki wakai onna no ko ni chiyahoya shite moraō nante amai wa yo. Sono buyobuyo no onaka. Doko kara mita tte tan-naru ojisan no kuse ni.*
Atsushi:	*Sonna tan-naru ojisan ni meromero datta no wa doko no doitsu da yo.*

☀ ☀ ☀

Yumi:	What got into you this afternoon? I was so embarrassed I could have died. Ogling all the girls in sight…
Atsushi:	I wondered what you've been pissed off about. So that's all it was.
Yumi:	Don't give me any "So that's all it was." You were simply disgusting.
Atsushi:	What's so bad about admiring some bright-eyed young women?

Yumi:	It gives me the creeps just thinking about it. Smirking away and your tongue hanging out…
Atsushi:	What about you? (You looked sort of fishy yourself.) You and the instructor were hitting it off pretty well.
Yumi:	That shows how much you know. The nerve! You're the one who got all flustered as soon as some young girl came by. And at your age! Boy, did you look stupid.
Atsushi:	Well, excuse *me*.
Yumi:	Really, you're fooling yourself if you think that young girls are going to make a fuss over you at your age. Look at that paunch! Whichever way you look at it, you're nothing but another guy who's over the hill.
Atsushi:	And who was it who fell head over heels for that over-the-hill guy?

じいっと／じっと (jītto/jitto) N

To stay fixed or motionless, especially when staring at something or when enduring something painful or difficult. While *jitto* emphasizes the condition of motionless concentration, *jītto* stresses the duration.

❑ そんなにじいっと見つめないで。

Sonna ni jītto mitsumenai de.

Stop staring at me like that.

❑ 子供はちっともじっとしていないから、休む間もないんです。

Kodomo wa chittomo jitto shite inai kara, yasumu ma mo nai n' desu.

My kids can't keep still, so I never have a moment's peace.

ぷりぷり (puripuri) B

To get angry, to be in a bad mood.

❑ ワイシャツに口紅がついていたって、女房はぷりぷり怒って
　 いるんですよ。

Waishatsu ni kuchibeni ga tsuite ita tte, nyōbō wa puripuri okotte iru n' desu yo.

My wife says there was lipstick on my shirt, and now she's hopping mad.

❑ 課長は朝からぷりぷりして物も言わないけど、一体*何が
　 あったんですか。

Kachō wa asa kara puripuri shite mono mo iwanai kedo, ittai nani ga atta n' desu ka.

The section chief has been grumpy and not saying much since morning. What on earth happened?

> ❊ *Ittai*: lit., "in one body, all in all"; here, colloquial "ever, on earth" expressing strong doubt.

ぴちぴち (pichipichi) G / N

(1) The sound or feeling of a small object bouncing or flapping in a lively manner. Often used to describe live fish. (2) By extension, a spirited, active person—usually a young woman who is full of vim and vigor.

❑ 魚はやっぱりぴちぴちと生きがいいのじゃないとおいしくな
　 いよね。

Sakana wa yappari pichipichi to iki ga ii no ja nai to oishiku nai yo ne.

You know, fish just doesn't taste good unless it's nice and fresh.

❏ 新入社員は、ぴちぴちしてまぶしいくらいだよ。

Shinnyū-shain wa, pichipichi shite mabushii kurai da yo.

Those new girls we've hired are so fresh-faced and bright-eyed that
you're almost blinded by the dazzle.

ぞうっと／ぞっと (zōtto/zotto) B

To shiver with sudden cold or fright so that one's hair seems to stand
on end. *Zōtto* is the more emphatic.

❏ 突然ぞうっと寒気が襲ってきたので熱を計ってみたら、9度
もあったんです。

*Totsuzen zōtto samuke ga osotte kita no de netsu o hakatte mitara, ku-
do mo atta n' desu.*

All of a sudden I came down with the chills, and when I took my
temperature, it said 39°C (102.2°F).

❏ 高所恐怖症だから、高層ビルの窓から下をのぞき込んだり
するとぞっとするの。

*Kōsho–kyōfu-shō da kara, kōsō-biru no mado kara shita o nozokikon-
dari suru to zotto suru no.*

I have acrophobia, so I get the jitters when I do anything like look
down from the window of a skyscraper.

にたにた (nitanita) B

To smirk, to display a sinister smile or grin. Used to describe a person
who seems to be hiding some secret, unseemly pleasure or scheme.

❏ にたにたしていないで、はっきり言ったらどうなの。

Nitanita shite inai de, hakkiri ittara dō na no.

Stop smirking and say what's on your mind (come out with it).

❏ 君、社長に向かってそのにたにた笑いは何だね、失礼だよ。

Kimi, shachō ni mukatte sono nitanita-warai wa nan da ne, shitsurei da yo.

Hey there. What do you think you're doing, smirking at the company president like that? It's downright rude.

いちゃいちゃ (ichaicha) B

Used to describe a couple engaging in a public display of affection, particularly when viewed as unsavory by others.

❏ 会社の中でいちゃいちゃしてるなんて、言語道断＊だよ。

Kaisha no naka de ichaicha shite 'ru nante, gongo-dōdan da yo.

It's simply outrageous the way those two make like little lovebirds right in the office.

❀ *Gongo-dōdan*: lit., "the way is closed to language"; unspeakably bad.

❏ パッケージ・ツアーも考えものだね。新婚さんにいちゃいちゃあてつけられて＊まいったよ。

Pakkēji-tsuā mo kangaemono da ne. Shinkon-san ni ichaicha atetsukerarete maitta yo.

You should think twice about going on a package tour. I got stuck with a bunch of spooning newlyweds.

❀ *Atetsukeru*: to annoy or do something out of spite; to parade or flaunt affectionate relations.

➡ Japanese tradition has long frowned on men and women holding hands, kissing, or showing affection in public. This is due in part to the influence of Confucianism, which held that boys and girls should be kept apart after the age of seven. Visit a park in Japan on a Sunday afternoon, though, and you will see that the younger generation is not taking this old moral code too seriously.

そわそわ (sowasowa) N / B

To be distracted, nervous, unable to settle down.

❑ さっきから時計ばかり気にして、そわそわしているけど、何か約束でもあるの。

Sakki kara tokei bakari ki ni shite, sowasowa shite 'ru kedo, nani ka yakusoku de mo aru no.

You keep looking at your watch and fidgeting. Do you have an appointment or something?

❑ どうもそわそわと落ち着かないと思ったら、高木さん、今日お見合いなんですって。

Dōmo sowasowa to ochitsukanai to omottara, Takagi-san, kyō omiai nan desu tte.

Mr. Takagi seemed to be on pins and needles. It turns out that he has an *omiai* today.

➥ Many Japanese still get married by means of arranged introductions called 見合い *miai* (or *omiai*). Men and women who are interested in meeting potential marriage partners give their résumés, called 釣り書き *tsurigaki*, together with photographs, to an acquaintance who has agreed to arrange the meeting. This person then finds couples with compatible family and educational backgrounds, occupations, assets, physical attributes, etc., exchanges the *tsurigaki* and photos, and suggests a meeting. Either party is free to decline at this stage. If both are interested, a time and place are set up for them to be introduced. (A good place to snoop on *omiai* in progress is the coffee shop of a luxury hotel on a weekend afternoon.) After the meeting, the couple usually go on a few dates by themselves, after which time they decide whether or not to continue meeting with the ultimate goal being marriage.

The phrase 見合い結婚 *miai kekkon* is often translated as "arranged marriage." This is misleading, though, since it suggests that the marriage is arranged by the family without the consent of the parties involved. While such marriages were once common in Japan, especially among the upper classes, nearly all people who take part in *omiai* today do so voluntarily. In recent years, 恋愛結婚 *ren'ai kekkon*—often translated as "love marriage"—has become by far the more common practice.

ちやほや (chiyahoya) B

To fuss over, spoil, butter up. Generally in a critical sense.

❏ おばあちゃん子でちやほやと育てられたから、彼はわがまま
   なところがあるんだよ。

*Obāchan-ko de chiyahoya to sodaterareta kara, kare wa wagamama
na tokoro ga aru n' da yo.*

He was spoiled by his grandmother (he was a grandma's boy) when
he was growing up, so now he's a bit selfish.

❏ 社長の娘だからとまわりがちやほやするから、ますます本人
   も増長＊するんだよ。

*Shachō no musume da kara to mawari ga chiyahoya suru kara, masu-
masu honnin mo zōchō suru n' da yo.*

Since she's the president's daughter and everyone makes a big fuss
over her, she's getting more and more stuck up.

❊ *Zōchō*: to grow gradually worse; to become increasingly arrogant.

ぶよぶよ (buyobuyo) B

Squishy, squelchy, flabby, puffy, bloated. Used to describe a soft,
liquid-filled object, especially one that is unpleasant to the touch or
sight.

❏ 天ぷらを揚げてたら油がはねて、手にぶよぶよの水ぶくれが
   できちゃったのよ。痛いわ。

*Tempura o agete 'tara abura ga hanete, te ni buyobuyo no mizubukure
ga dekichatta no yo. Itai wa.*

I got spattered with oil when I was cooking tempura, and now I
have a big, squishy blister on my hand. My, does it hurt.

❏ いくら温泉が気持ちいいからといっても、そんなに入ってた
　らふやけて*ぶよぶよになるぞ。

Ikura onsen ga kimochi ii kara to itte mo, sonna ni haitte 'tara fuyakete buyobuyo ni naru zo.

I know it feels good to be soaking yourself in the hot spring, but you're going to get waterlogged if you stay in too long.

　　※ *Fuyakeru:* to swell up, get soggy.

めろめろ (meromero)　N / B

Limp, floppy, spineless, unable to stand up straight. Often used to criticize someone's weakness or lack of resolve.

❏ あの会社はワンマン社長が倒れて、今めろめろになってい
　るみたいだよ。

Ano kaisha wa wanman-shachō ga taorete, ima meromero ni natte iru mitai da yo.

Ever since its all-powerful president fell ill, that company has sort of come apart at the seams.

❏ 恵子は今彼にめろめろだから、何を言っても耳に入らない
　わよ。

Keiko wa ima kare ni meromero da kara, nani o itte mo mimi ni hairanai wa yo.

Right now Keiko is all moony (has gone cuckoo) over him. No matter what you say to her, it goes in one ear and out the other.

Quiz

Fill in the blanks with one of the words studied in this chapter: じ いっと／じっと jītto/jitto, ぷりぷり puripuri, ぴちぴち pichipichi, ぞうっと／ぞっと zōtto/zotto, にたにた nitanita, いちゃいちゃ ichaicha, そわそわ sowasowa, ちやほや chiyahoya, ぶよぶよ buyobuyo, めろめろ meromero. There are at least two sentences for each word. Answers are on page 219.

1 そんなに（　　　　　）見ないでよ、恥ずかしいから。

Sonna ni (　　　　) minai de yo, hazukashii kara.

Don't stare at me like that. It's embarrassing.

2 あの人はちょっとしたことでも（　　　　）腹を立てるんだ。

Ano hito wa chotto shita koto de mo (　　　　) hara o tateru n' da.

He seems to get mad at the slightest thing.

3 みんな（　　　　）していてうらやましいね。

Minna (　　　　) shite ite urayamashii ne.

You're all so full of life I'm practically envious.

4 あの飛行機にもし乗っていたらと思うと今でも（　　　　）鳥肌が立つよ。

Ano hikōki ni moshi notte itara to omou to ima de mo (　　　　) tori-hada ga tatsu.

147

It still gives me goose bumps to think that I might have been on that plane.

5 (　　　　) 笑_{わら}ってばかりで、気味_{きみ}が悪_{わる}いなあ。

(　　　　) *waratte bakari de, kimi ga warui naa.*

The way he keeps smirking all the time gives me the creeps.

6 人前_{ひとまえ}で (　　　　) としちゃって、恥_はずかしくないのかしら。

Hitomae de (　　　　) to shichatte, hazukashiku nai no kashira.

I wonder that they don't feel embarrassed at all, making out in public like that.

7 さっきから (　　　　) と落_おち着_つかないね。どうしたの？

Sakki kara (　　　　) to ochitsukanai ne. Dō shita no?

You've been fidgeting for some time now. What's up?

8 あの子_こ、(　　　　) と育_{そだ}てられたから、わがままになっちゃって。

Ano ko, (　　　　) to sodaterareta kara, wagamama ni natchatte.

He was raised spoiled, and he's turned into a selfish kid.

9 やけどして皮膚_{ひふ}が (　　　　) になっちゃった。

Yakedo shite hifu ga (　　　　) ni natchatta.

I burned myself and now have this big old blister.

10 結局会議_{けっきょくかいぎ}で反論_{はんろん}されたら (　　　　) だったね。

Kekkyoku kaigi de hanron saretara (　　　　) datta ne.

When he ran into some opposition at the meeting, he completely lost it.

11 昨日_{きのう}は具合_{ぐあい}が悪_{わる}くて一日中家_{いちにちじゅういえ}で (　　　　) していたんだ。

Kinō wa guai ga warukute ichinichi-jū ie de (   ) shite ita n' da.

Yesterday I wasn't feeling well and spent the whole day at home doing nothing (just loafing around, killing time).

12 どういうわけか、彼女、(   )怒っているんだ。

Dō iu wake ka, kanojo (   ) okotte iru n' da.

I don't know what's got into her, but she's pretty hot under the collar.

13 (   )と生きのいい魚じゃないと、生で食べる気がしないな。

(   ) to iki no ii sakana ja nai to, nama de taberu ki ga shinai na.

I don't feel like eating raw fish unless it's absolutely fresh.

14 あの映画、(   )するような怖い結末だったね。

Ano eiga, (   ) suru yō na kowai ketsumatsu datta ne.

Boy, that movie really had a scary (hair-raising) ending.

15 あの子どうも (   ) していると思ったら、いたずらしてたのよ。

Ano ko dōmo (   ) shite iru to omottara, itazura shite 'ta no yo.

I thought the kid had a funny smile on his face. He had been up to no good.

16 満員電車の中で (   )されると迷惑だね。

Man'in-densha no naka de (   ) sareru to meiwaku da ne.

It's a little much when you're caught in a jam-packed train with a couple making out.

17 何年やっていても、舞台に出る前は(   )するんだ。

Nannen yatte ite mo, butai ni deru mae wa (   ) suru n' da.

No matter how many years you've been doing it, appearing on the
    stage still puts you on edge.

18 美人は得だな、みんなに（　　　　）されて。

Bijin wa toku da na, minna ni (　　　　) sarete.

Beautiful women are so lucky, being fussed over all the time.

19 運動不足でお腹が（　　　　）だ。

Undō-busoku de onaka ga (　　　　) da.

Not getting any excercise, I'm getting flabby around the middle.

20 彼ったら、あの女の人に（　　　　）なのよ。

Kare ttara, ano onna no hito ni (　　　　) na no yo.

He's a case, I tell you. He's completely lost his head over her.

SMOOTHING THINGS OVER

Mr. and Mrs. Hasegawa are approaching their mid-thirties. Before going to sleep one Sunday night, they have a talk in the bedroom.

京子　「ねえ、あなた、この頃(ごろ)**つるつる**になってきたような気(き)がしない？」

隆　　「なっ、何(なん)だよ急(きゅう)に。」(と、近頃薄(ちかごろうす)くなってきた頭(あたま)に思(おも)わず手(て)をやる)

京子　**「てかてか**っていうほどでもないけどさ。」

隆　　「冗談(じょうだん)じゃないよ。それはない*よ。」

京子　「そうかしら。お手当(てあ)ては早(はや)め早(はや)めが肝心(かんじん)なのよね。最近(さいきん)いいのが出(で)てるのよ。ちょっと高(たか)いけど。お隣(となり)も使(つか)っていらっしゃるんですって。」

隆　　「ふうん。」

京子　「朝(あさ)と晩(ばん)、**せっせと**付(つ)けて**ぴしゃぴしゃ**たたくようにするといいんですって。」

隆　　「どのくらいで効(き)くのかなあ。」

京子　「そりゃあ、**めきめき**というわけにはいかないでしょうけど。**じわじわ**効(き)いてくるんじゃない？」

隆　　「高(たか)いっていくら？」

京子　「うふふ。実(じつ)はね、もう買(か)っちゃったんだ。お客様(きゃくさま)のお肌(はだ)に**ぴったり**ですって勧(すす)められたんだもん。」

隆　　「何(なん)だよそれ。」

京子　「あら、美顔(びがん)クリームに決(き)まってるじゃない。**しっとりつやつや**になったでしょう。」

隆　　「おいおい、いくらだよ。」

京子　「2万円(まんえん)。**すべすべ**のお肌(はだ)が買(か)えると思(おも)えば安(やす)いものよね、あなた。」

❋ *Sore wa nai*: more empathic version of *sonna koto wa nai* ("it's nothing like that," "no way!").

Kyōko:	*Nē, anata, konogoro tsurutsuru ni natte kita yō na ki ga shinai?*
Takashi:	*Na——, nan da yo kyū ni.* (to, chikagoro usuku natte kita atama ni omowazu te o yaru)
Kyōko:	*Tekateka tte iu hodo de mo nai kedo sa.*
Takashi:	*Jōdan ja nai yo. Sore wa nai yo.*
Kyōko:	*Sō kashira. Oteate wa hayame-hayame ga kanjin na no yo ne. Saikin ii no ga dete 'ru no yo. Chotto takai kedo. Otonari mo tsukatte irassharu n' desu tte.*
Takashi:	*Fūn.*
Kyōko:	*Asa to ban, sesseto tsukete pishapisha tataku yō ni suru to ii n' desu tte.*
Takashi:	*Dono kurai de kiku no ka nā.*
Kyōko:	*Soryā, mekimeki to iu wake ni wa ikanai deshō kedo. Jiwa-jiwa kiite kuru n' ja nai?*
Takashi:	*Takai tte ikura?*
Kyōko:	*Ufufu. Jitsu wa ne, mō katchatta n' da. Okyaku-sama no ohada ni pittari desu tte susumerareta n' da mon.*
Takashi:	*Nan da yo sore.*
Kyōko:	*Ara, bigan-kurīmu ni kimatte 'ru ja nai. Shittori tsuyatsuya ni natta deshō.*
Takashi:	*Oioi, ikura da yo.*
Kyōko:	*Ni-man'en. Subesube no ohada ga kaeru to omoeba yasui mono yo ne, anata.*

Kyōko: Say, honey. Haven't you noticed how much smoother it's become these days, sort of like a billiard ball?

Takashi: Wha—, what brings that on? (Without thinking, he touches his recently thinning hair.)

Kyōko: I wouldn't go so far as to call it slick, though.

Takashi: You've got to be kidding! It's not that bad!

Kyōko: You think so? It's awfully important to start treatment as soon as possible. Some good stuff has come out lately. It's a little expensive, but I hear our next-door neighbor is using it.

Takashi: Hmm.

Kyōko: They say it works if you keep steadily at it every morning and night, practically slapping it on.

Takashi: I wonder how long it takes to work.

Kyōko: It's not by leaps and bounds, I imagine. It probably more like slow and steady.

Takashi: How expensive is "expensive"?

Kyōko: Hee-hee. As a matter of fact, I've already bought some. They *recommended* it to me. Said it would be perfect for my skin.

Takashi: Bought some! What did you buy?

Kyōko: Why, facial cream, of course. Doesn't my skin look so much moister and glowing?

Takashi: For crying out loud! How much did it cost?

Kyōko: Twenty thousand yen. Don't you think that's a bargain for nice, smooth skin, honey?

つるつる (tsurutsuru) G / N / B

(1) Smooth, shiny, slick (G/N/B). (2) To slide smoothly across a flat surface (N). (3) The sound or feeling of slurping or ingesting something that has a smooth surface. Often used to describe the eating of soba, udon, or other noodlelike food (N).

❏ お肌がつるつるになるっていうからこのクリームを買ったのに、かぶれちゃったわ。

Ohada ga tsurutsuru ni naru tte iu kara kono kurīmu o katta no ni, kaburechatta wa.

I bought this cream because they said it would make my skin nice and smooth. Instead, I broke out in a rash.

❏ きのうの雪が凍って道路がつるつるだから、足元に気をつけてね。

Kinō no yuki ga kōtte dōro ga tsurutsuru da kara, ashimoto ni ki o tsukete ne.

Yesterday's snow has turned to ice. The streets are slippery, so watch your step.

❏ 夏は冷や麦をつるつるやるっていうのが最高だね。

Natsu wa hiyamugi o tsurutsuru yaru tte iu no ga saikō da ne.

In summer there's nothing like slurping down some nice cool *hiya-mugi* (thin *udon* served with water and ice).

➡ Japan is a noodle mecca. Even the smallest towns have shops selling ラーメン *rāmen* (Chinese noodles served in a hot broth), and the fried chow mein called 焼きそば *yakisoba* is often sold from stalls at neighborhood festivals and other public events. Italian spaghetti is popular as well. Besides these recent imports, Japan has two main types of indigenous noodles: そば *soba* and うどん *udon.*

Soba is made from buckwheat flour combined with plain wheat flour, yams, egg whites, and other ingredients. The batter is mixed with water and rolled into a flat dough, which is then sliced into thin strips to form the noodles. It can be eaten with each mouthful dipped into a broth flavored with soy sauce, or it may be served in hot broth in a wide-brimmed bowl. Soba is particularly popular in the Kantō region.

Udon is prepared in the same way as *soba*, but instead of buckwheat flour the raw material is plain wheat flour. Its origins in Japan are said to date back to the Nara Period (701–784), when wonton was introduced from China. *Udon* noodles are fatter and whiter than *soba*, but they are eaten in much the same way. In Kansai, *udon* is more popular than *soba*.

Two particularly tasty versions of *udon* that are popular during the hot summer months are 冷や麦 *hiyamugi* and そうめん *sōmen*. Usually sold in dry form like spaghetti, the noodles are boiled in water and then cooled with ice or cold water. Then they are dipped into a soy-sauce-flavored broth and eaten. *Hiyamugi* noodles are a bit fatter than *sōmen*, and they are often eaten from a bowl of cold water.

Proper Japanese manners call for a hearty slurping noise when eating noodles. Noodles served in a hot broth become gooey and lose their flavor if they're left standing, so people generally like to eat them while they are still piping hot. To avoid burning the mouth, the Japanese have developed the habit of inhaling air with the noodles. This cools off the food and lets you savor the broth at the same time. If you eat noodles without accompanying noises, people will think you don't like the taste. (Basically, this rule applies only to noodles. With other kinds of food, loud munching or smacking noises are frowned upon.)

てかてか (tekateka) N / B

The shiny appearance of a smooth surface. Often in reference to something cheap-looking.

❏ 制服のズボンのお尻がすりきれててかてかになっちゃった。

Seifuku no zubon no oshiri ga surikirete tekateka ni natchatta.

The seat of my uniform pants has worn so thin it's started to shine.

❏ ポマードでてかてかの頭なんて、今時はやらないわよね。

Pomādo de tekateka no atama nante, ima-doki hayaranai wa yo ne.

In this day and age *nobody* slicks down his hair with hair oil (pomade) anymore.

せっせと (sesseto) G / N

With steady and uninterrupted diligence.

❏ せっせと貯金をしても、こう金利が低くてはねえ。

Sesseto chōkin o shite mo, kō kinri ga hikukute wa nē.

I put money in the bank as regular as clockwork, but with the interest rates so low, you know…

❏ せっせと立ち働いているお母さんの姿を見たら、涙が出たわ。

Sesseto tachihataraite iru okāsan no sugata o mitara, namida ga deta wa.

Seeing my mother working as busy as a bee, I couldn't keep the tears from my eyes.

ぴしゃぴしゃ (pishapisha) N

The sound or feeling of something soft (like drops of water) and often flat (such as the palm of the hand) hitting against a soft or wet surface.

❏ 子供のお尻をぴしゃぴしゃたたいてお仕置きするような親なんて、近頃いなくなったね。

Kodomo no oshiri o pishapisha tataite oshioki suru yō na oya nante, chikagoro inaku natta ne.

There aren't any parents around these days who discipline their children by giving their little behinds a good spanking.

❏ 雨の日はぴしゃぴしゃはねをあげちゃう*から、外に出るの
がおっくうなのよね。

*Ame no hi wa pishapisha hane o agechau kara, soto ni deru no ga okkū
na no yo ne.*

I really hate going out on rainy days because my legs get all spattered
with water.

> ❊ *Hane o ageru*: lit., "to raise jumps"; i.e., to create splashes, to splash, to spat-
> ter (oneself or one's own clothing).

めきめき (mekimeki) G

Used to describe quick progress, growth, recovery, etc.

❏ 書道を始めたとは聞いてたけど、あんまりめきめき腕が上
がった*んで驚いたよ。

*Shodō o hajimeta to wa kiite 'ta kedo, anmari mekimeki ude ga agatta
n' de odoroita yo.*

I heard she'd started doing calligraphy, but I was really surprised by
how fast she'd gotten the hang of it.

> ❊ *Ude ga agaru*: to have one's skills improve in a practical skill or art.

❏ 小学校の時には背が低い方だったんだけど、中学に入って
からめきめき伸びたんだ。

*Shōgakkō no toki ni wa se ga hikui hō datta n' da kedo, chūgaku ni
haitte kara mekimeki nobita n' da.*

I was short all through elementary school, but after entering junior
high I shot up like a beanstalk.

じわじわ (jiwajiwa) N

Growing or progressing slowly but steadily.

❑ 冬なのに、今日は日中じわじわと汗ばむような陽気だったね。

Fuyu na no ni, kyō wa nitchū jiwajiwa to asebamu yō na yōki datta ne.

Although it's winter, the weather today was so fine during the day-
    time that you actually started to work up a sweat.

❑ 漢方薬は即効性はないけど、じわじわきいてきて副作用が
    少ないんですって。

*Kanpō-yaku wa sokkō-sei wa nai kedo, jiwajiwa kiite kite fuku-sayō ga
    sukunai n' desu tte.*

They say Chinese herbal medicine isn't quick to take effect, but it
    works little by little and doesn't have many side effects.

ぴったり／ぴたり (pittari/pitari) G / N

(1) Perfectly matched, on target, just right, completely suitable
(G/N). (2) Solidly attached, tightly closed (N). (3) Used to describe
a continuous action that comes to a complete or sudden stop (N).
The meanings of *pittari* and *pitari* are very similar, with *pittari* used
for emphasis and *pitari* when the meaning is "on target." The choice
for "completely suitable" is usually *pittari*. When the word is used as
an adjectival verb followed by *da* or *na*, only the *pittari* form is possible.

❑ この背広、まるであつらえたように君にぴったりだね。

Kono sebiro, maru de atsuraeta yō ni kimi ni pittari da ne.

That suit fits you so well it looks like it was tailor-made.

❏ あの占い師は何でもぴたりと当てちゃうんですって。

Ano uranai-shi wa nan de mo pitari to atechau n' desu tte.

They say that fortune-teller hits the nail on the head about everything (every time).

❏ 車にはったステッカーが、ぴったりとくっついて離れないの。困るわ。

Kuruma ni hatta sutekkā ga, pittari to kuttsuite hanarenai no. Komaru wa.

The sticker on my car is stuck on so hard that it just won't come off. Darn!

❏ 横山さん、医者に注意されてから、タバコをぴたりとやめたらしいよ。

Yokoyama-san, isha ni chūi sarete kara, tabako o pitari to yameta rashii yo.

Apparently Mr. Yokoyama quit smoking cold turkey as soon as he was warned by his doctor.

しっとり (shittori) G

(1) Moist. Often used to describe skin that is soft to the touch. (2) Calm, quiet, relaxed, soothing. Can be used to describe people, the atmosphere of a place, etc. When describing a woman, *shittori* suggests that she is graceful, calm, gentle.

❏ 私は乾燥肌だから、久美子さんみたいなしっとりした潤いのある肌にあこがれるわ。

Watashi wa kansō-hada da kara, Kumiko-san mitai na shittori shita uruoi no aru hada ni akogareru wa.

My skin is the dry type, so I really envy moist, smooth skin like yours, Kumiko.

❏ たまには仕事を離れて温泉にでもつかって、しっとりとした気分を味わいたいものだね。

Tama ni wa shigoto o hanarete onsen ni de mo tsukatte, shittori to shita kibun o ajiwaitai mono da ne.

Sometimes I want to get away from work, soak in some hot springs, and enjoy a mood of complete tranquillity.

❏ 康子さんは、着物の似合うしっとりとした雰囲気の人だね。

Yasuko-san wa, kimono no niau shittori to shita fun'iki no hito da ne.

Yasuko has an air of gentle grace, so a kimono looks good on her.

つやつや (tsuyatsuya) G

Shining, glistening, sparkling. Often used to describe skin, hair, feathers, leather, etc.

❏ つやつやした黒い髪のことを、からすのぬれ羽色っていうのよ。

Tsuyatsuya shita kuroi kami no koto o, karasu no nureba-iro tte iu no yo.

The phrase "the color of wet raven feathers" is used to describe beautifully shiny black hair.

❏ いつもつやつやの肌をしていらっしゃるけれど、何かお手入れの秘けつがあるんですか。

Itsumo tsuyatsuya no hada o shite irassharu keredo, nani ka oteire no hiketsu ga aru n' desu ka.

Your skin is always glowing. Do you have some secret method of skin care?

すべすべ (subesube) G

Smooth and pleasing to the touch.

❑ ハンドクリームをぬって寝れば、水仕事で荒れた手もすべすべになりますよ。

Hando-kurīmu o nutte nereba, mizu-shigoto de areta te mo subesube ni narimasu yo.

If you put on some hand cream before you go to sleep, your dishpan hands will become nice and smooth.

❑ 柔らかくてすべすべで、まるで赤ちゃんのような肌ですね。

Yawarakakute subesube de, maru de akachan no yō na hada desu ne.

Your skin is so white and soft and delicate, just like a baby's.

❑ この建物、ずいぶん古いんでしょうね。階段の手すりもすべすべになっていますからね。

Kono tatemono, zuibun furui n' deshō ne. Kaidan no tesuri mo subesube ni natte imasu kara ne.

This building must be very old. Even the banisters have been worn smooth.

Quiz

Fill in the blanks with one of the words studied in this chapter: つ るつる tsurutsuru, てかてか tekateka, せっせと sesseto, ぴしゃぴ しゃ pishapisha, めきめき mekimeki, じわじわ jiwajiwa, ぴったり／ぴ たり pittari/pitari, しっとり shittori, つやつや tsuyatsuya, すべすべ subesube. There are at least two sentences for each word. Answers are on page 220.

1 路面が凍って（　　　　　）すべる。

Romen ga kōtte (　　　　) suberu.

The road is frozen and slippery.

2 ズボンのお尻が（　　　　　）だから、もう買いかえたらどう かしら。

Zubon no oshiri ga (　　　　) da kara, mō kaikaetara dō kashira.

The seat of your pants has started to shine. Don't you think you should buy a new pair?

3 （　　　　　）歩いて、少しやせなくちゃ。

(　　　　) aruite, sukoshi yasenakucha.

I've got to do some brisk walking and lose weight.

4 ローションはお肌に（　　　　　）たたくようにつけましょう。

Rōshon wa ohada ni (　　　　) tataku yō ni tsukemashō.

Lotion should be applied by patting it on the skin.

163

Quiz

5 語学というのは、そんなに短期間に（　　　　　）できるよう
にはなりませんよ。

Gogaku to iu no wa, sonna ni tankikan ni (　　　　) dekiru yō ni wa narimasen yo.

Language is not something you can expect to make huge progress in within such a short time.

6 スープを飲んだら、辛さが（　　　　）口の中に広がってき
た。

Sūpu o nondara, karasa ga (　　　) kuchi no naka ni hirogatte kita.

When I drank the soup, the spicy flavor slowly spread throughout my mouth.

7 ふたを（　　　　）と閉めて、空気が入らないようにしてね。

Futa o (　　　) to shimete, kūki ga hairanai yō ni shite ne.

Close the lid perfectly tight so that no air gets inside, okay.

8 この乳液をつけると、かさかさの肌も（　　　　）として気
持ちがいいわよ。

Kono nyūeki o tsukeru to, kasakasa no hada mo (　　　　) to shite kimochi ga ii wa yo.

When you apply this lotion, even rough, dry skin becomes moist and smooth, and it feels really wonderful.

9 夕べあんなに飲んだのに、（　　　　）した顔で元気に現れ
たわ。

Yūbe anna ni nonda no ni, (　　　) shita kao de genki ni arawareta wa.

Even though he drank that much last night, he showed up full of energy and with a glowing face.

10 この温泉、肌が（　　　　）になるね。

Kono onsen, hada ga (   ) ni naru ne.

At this hot spring your skin becomes slick and smooth.

11 床<ruby>ゆか<rt></rt></ruby>にワックスをかけたばかりで（   ）だから気<ruby><rt>き</rt></ruby>をつけたほうがいいよ。

Yuka ni wakkusu o kaketa bakari de (   ) da kara ki o tsuketa hō ga ii yo.

The floor has just been waxed and is as slick as ice. Watch your step.

12 顔<ruby><rt>かお</rt></ruby>が（   ）に光<ruby><rt>ひか</rt></ruby>っているけど、どうしたの？

Kao ga (   ) ni hikatte iru kedo, dō shita no?

Your face is practically glistening. What happened?

13 （   ）お小遣<ruby><rt>こづか</rt></ruby>いをためちゃって、何<ruby><rt>なに</rt></ruby>に使<ruby><rt>つか</rt></ruby>うの？

(   ) okozukai o tamechatte, nani ni tsukau no?

Squirreling away your allowance as fast as you can—how are you going to use it?

14 雨<ruby><rt>あめ</rt></ruby>の中<ruby><rt>なか</rt></ruby>を歩<ruby><rt>ある</rt></ruby>いていたら、（   ）はねをあげちゃってズボンのすそが汚<ruby><rt>よご</rt></ruby>れちゃったわ。

Ame no naka o aruite itara, (   ) hane o agechatte zubon no suso ga yogorechatta wa.

Walking in the rain, I splashed water on my pant cuffs and got them dirty.

15 彼<ruby><rt>かれ</rt></ruby>はチェスの才能<ruby><rt>さいのう</rt></ruby>があるんですよ、あんなに（   ）上<ruby><rt>じょう</rt></ruby>達<ruby><rt>たつ</rt></ruby>するんですから。

Kare wa chesu no sainō ga aru n' desu yo, anna ni (   ) jōtatsu suru n' desu kara.

He has a knack for chess, all right. Look how rapidly he has progressed.

16 二位の走者が（　　　　　）と追いついてきた。

Ni-i no sōsha ga (　　　　) to oitsuite kita.

Little by little the second-place runner caught up.

17 君に（　　　　　）の仕事が見つかってよかったね。

Kimi ni (　　　　) no shigoto ga mitsukatte yokatta ne.

I'm glad you found a job that suits you to a T.

18 雨上がりには木々が（　　　　　）ぬれて、緑が一段ときれいだね。

Ameagari ni wa kigi ga (　　　　) nurete, midori ga ichidan to kirei da ne.

After it rains, the trees are covered with a thin layer of moisture, and the greenery is even more beautiful than before.

19 髪が（　　　　　）に光っていてうらやましいわ。

Kami ga (　　　　) ni hikatte ite urayamashii wa.

Your hair is practically shining. I'm so envious.

20 この紙は（　　　　）のほうが表です。

Kono kami wa (　　　　) no hō ga omote desu.

The slick side of this paper is the front.

"PRETTY WOMAN"

Two female office workers, Yoshiko Sugiyama and Kaori Yasuda, are in a coffee shop talking about movies.

良子　「『プリティ・ウーマン』のDVDを借りたんですって？　どうだった？」

香織　「すっごくよかったわよ。おすすめだわ。」

良子　「どんなところが？」

香織　「**はらはらどきどき**の連続なのよ。それに何といってもリチャード・ギアがカッコイイの！」

良子　「彼氏*と見たんでしょ。」

香織　「まあね。とにかく、ジュリア・ロバーツもかわいいし。もう**ぼうっと**しちゃったわよ。」

良子　「ふうん。」

香織　「最初は**ぱっと**しない彼女がさあ、見違えるようにきれいになっちゃうのよね。」

良子　「やっぱり女は男次第ってことなのかしら。」

香織　「ラストがまたいいのよ。オープン・カーでバラの花を持って彼女を迎えにいくんだけどさ。リチャード・ギアには**うっとり**よね。」

良子　「いいなあ、香織は。**しっかり**した彼もいるしさ。」

香織　「あれはやめたわ。**はっきり**言ってもう**うんざり**。」

良子　「なぜ？」

香織　「DVDの後、何を食べに行ったと思う？　焼き肉定食†よ。**がばがば**ビールは飲むし。もう最低。**がっくり**よ。」

❖ *Kareshi*: boyfriend.

† *Yakiniku-teishoku*: see note following English translation (p.170).

Yoshiko: *"Puritī-ūman" no dībuidī o karita n' desu tte? Dō datta?*

Kaori: *Sugoku yokatta wa yo. Osusume da wa.*

Yoshiko: *Donna tokoro ga?*

Kaori: *Harahara dokidoki no renzoku na no yo. Sore ni nan to itte mo Richādo Gia ga kakko ii no!*

Yoshiko: *Kareshi to mita n' desho.*

Kaori: *Mā ne. Tonikaku, Juria Robātsu mo kawaii shi. Mō pōtto shichatta wa yo.*

Yoshiko: *Fūn.*

Kaori: *Saisho wa patto shinai kanojo ga sā, michigaeru yō ni kirei ni natchau no yo ne.*

Yoshiko: *Yappari onna wa otoko-shidai tte koto na no kashira.*

Kaori: *Rasuto ga mata ii no yo. Ōpun-kā de bara no hana o motte kanojo o mukae ni iku n' da kedo sa. Richādo Gia ni wa uttori yo ne.*

Yoshiko: *Ii nā, Kaori wa. Shikkari shita kare mo iru shi sa.*

Kaori: *Are wa yameta wa. Hakkiri itte mō unzari.*

Yoshiko: *Naze?*

Kaori: *Dībuidī no ato, nani o tabe ni itta to omou? Yakiniku-teishoku yo. Gabagaba bīru wa nomu shi. Mō saitei. Gakkuri yo.*

* * *

Yoshiko: You rented the DVD for "Pretty Woman"? How was it?

Kaori: Absolutely fantastic. I highly recommend it.

Yoshiko: What was so good about it?

Kaori: It keeps you on the edge of your seat from beginning to end. And best of all, Richard Gere is just so cool!

Yoshiko: You watched it with your boyfriend, right?

Kaori: Yeah, well… Anyhow, Julia Roberts is cute, too. I was practically in a daze.

Yoshiko: Hmm.

Kaori: At first she's not much to speak of, but later on she's so beautiful you'd hardly recognize her.

Yoshiko: So maybe it's true that a woman is only as good as her man.

Kaori: The last scene was good, too. He comes in this convertible with some roses to pick her up. Richard Gere really knocks me out.

Yoshiko: How neat for you, Kaori. And you've got such a reliable boyfriend, too.

Kaori: No, I dumped him. To tell you the truth, I just got fed up.

Yoshiko: How come?

Kaori: After the DVD, guess what we went out to eat? *Yakiniku-teishoku,* that's what. And he was guzzling beer on top of that. What a bummer!

➡ The most popular restaurants for a young man to take his girlfriend in Japan are French or Italian, for European cuisine has a stylish, sophisticated image. She's likely to be disappointed if he instead chooses ラーメン *rāmen* "Chinese noodles," ギョーザ *gyōza* "meat dumplings," or 焼き肉定食 *yakiniku-teishoku* "barbecued beef set"; in other words, inexpensive food, served in inelegant surroundings.

A *yakiniku-teishoku* consists of thinly sliced Korean-style barbecued beef accompanied by rice, soup, and perhaps some onions or vegetables. Popular with office workers on their lunch break, *teishoku* sets can be prepared and eaten quickly and are cheaper than à la carte. Other common *teishoku* are 焼き魚定食 *yakizakana-teishoku* "fried fish set" and とんかつ定食 *tonkatsu-teishoku* "pork cutlet set."

はらはら (harahara) N / B

(1) To worry or fret about how things will turn out. Primarily used to describe a passive observer's anxiety at watching something that is dangerous or frightening (N/B). (2) The feeling or appearance of small, light objects—flower petals, leaves, rain, dewdrops, tears—falling gently a few at a time. In this sense, *harahara* often suggests a melancholy feeling about the passage of time (N).

❏ 君の運転にははらはらさせられるよ。ちっともバックミラーを見ていないんだもの。

Kimi no unten ni wa harahara saserareru yo. Chittomo bakku-mirā o mite inai n' da mono.

Your driving scares me to death. You never even glance at the rearview mirror.

❏ はらはらと桜の花が散るのを見ていると、この世の無常を感じるね。

Harahara to sakura no hana ga chiru no o mite iru to, kono yo no mujō o kanjiru ne.

Watching the cherry blossoms flutter down makes you realize how fleeting life is.

どきどき (dokidoki) G / N / B

The sound or feeling of rapid, pounding heartbeats caused by worry, fear, surprise, sudden exercise, or excited expectation. While *harahara* expresses one's nervousness about some event occurring outside oneself, *dokidoki* refers to one's reaction to something one is directly involved in.

❏ 駅の階段を駆け上がっただけでどきどきするなんて、我ながら情け無いよ。

Eki no kaidan o kakeagatta dake de dokidoki suru nante, ware-nagara nasake-nai yo.

It's pretty sad, even if I do say so myself, the way my heart starts pounding when I just run up the stairs at the train station.

❑ 君に振られるんじゃないかと思って、内心どきどきしていたんだ。

Kimi ni furareru n' ja nai ka to omotte, naishin dokidoki shite ita n' da.

I was beside myself with worry, thinking you were going to jilt me.

ぽうっと (pōtto) G / N

(1) To be so distracted or obsessed with something that you don't notice what is happening right in front of you (N). (2) A bright, reddish appearance (G/N). In either sense, *pōtto* often suggests the feeling of blood rushing to one's head.

❑ 田村さん、ぽうっとしていると思ったら、新入社員の村上さんに一目ぼれしたらしいのよ。

Tamura-san, pōtto shite iru to omottara, shin'nyū-shain no Murakami-san ni hitome-bore shita rashii no yo.

I had the feeling Miss Tamura was going around in a daze. Apparently she fell for the new employee, Mr. Murakami, at first sight.

❑ 私、お酒は弱いんです。すぐぽうっと顔が赤くなっちゃって。

Watashi, osake wa yowai n' desu. Sugu pōtto kao ga akaku natchatte.

I'm not a very good drinker. My face immediately turns as red as a beet.

ぱっと／ぱあっと (patto/pātto) G / N

(1) Showy, gaudy, spectacular. In this meaning, *patto* is usually used in the negative form, *patto shinai,* meaning dull, somber, unsatisfactory. However, the version with the long vowel, *pātto,* does not have the negative form (G/N). (2) A quick or sudden motion or change (N). (3) A spreading or widening action (N).

❏ 営業成績は今ひとつ*ぱっとしないが、今夜はぱあっと派手に繰り出そう†、諸君。

Eigyō-seiseki wa ima-hitotsu patto shinai ga, kon'ya wa pātto hade ni kuridasō, shokun.

Our sales aren't much to brag about, boys, but let's go out tonight and paint the town red anyway.

    ❊ *Ima-hitotsu:* not quite enough, lacking.

    † *Kuridasu:* to flock, turn out in force.

❏ 子供は道路でもぱっととび出すから危ないわね。

Kodomo wa dōro de mo patto tobidasu kara abunai wa ne.

It's dangerous how children dash out into the street.

❏ 人の噂はぱっと広まるから怖いよ。

Hito no uwasa wa patto hiromaru kara kowai yo.

It's frightening how fast gossip spreads.

うっとり (uttori) G

To be enraptured by the beauty of something.

❏ 玉三郎*の舞台はやっぱりいいわね。あまりの美しさにうっとり見とれちゃったわ。

Tamasaburō no butai wa yappari ii wa ne. Amari no utsukushisa ni uttori mitorechatta wa.

Tamasaburō's performances really are great. I was overwhelmed by the sheer beauty of it.

> ❀ *Tamasaburō*: Bandō (坂東) Tamasaburō, Kabuki actor specializing in female roles, born 1950; the fifth in a line of actors using this name since the early nineteenth century.

❑ 育子さんはピアノがすごく上手なのよ。彼女のショパンなんてうっとりと聴きほれるわ。

Ikuko-san wa piano ga sugoku jōzu na no yo. Kanojo no Shopan nante uttori to kikihoreru wa.

Ikuko is a fantastic pianist. Listening to her Chopin, I practically go into a trance.

しっかり (shikkari) G/N/B

(1) To have a solid foundation, structure, connection, etc. (G/N). (2) Trustworthy, dependable, solid. Often used to describe a person's body, spirit, personality, intelligence, ideas, etc. Can also describe a company, source of information, or many other things (G/N). *Shikkari* sometimes refers sarcastically to a crafty or stingy person (B). (3) Referring to action and behavior: well, sufficiently, solidly, diligently (G). (4) A large number or amount (G/N).

❑ マンション選びのポイントは、まず構造がしっかりしているかどうかですよ。

Manshon-erabi no pointo wa, mazu kōzō ga shikkari shite iru ka dō ka desu yo.

The first thing you should check before buying a condominium is how solidly it's built.

❏ お父さん、しっかりしてよ。酔っぱらって玄関で寝ちゃった
ら風邪ひくわよ。

*Otōsan, shikkari shite yo. Yopparatte genkan de nechattara kaze hiku
wa yo.*

Pull yourself together, Dad. You'll catch a cold if you lie down
drunk like that in the entranceway.

❏ しっかりした会社に勤めていれば不況になっても安心です
ね。

*Shikkari shita kaisha ni tsutomete ireba fukyō ni natte mo anshin desu
ne.*

If you work for a solid company, you won't have to worry about a
faltering economy.

❏ 女房のやつ、しっかり者でね、この5年間に100万もヘソク
リしてたんだぜ。

*Nyōbō no yatsu, shikkari-mono de ne, kono go-nenkan ni hyaku-man
mo hesokuri shite 'ta n' da ze.*

My old lady is a real tightwad. In just the past five years, man, she's
stashed away all of a million yen in pin money.

❏ 学生時代にもっとしっかりと勉強しておくべきだったよ。

Gakusei-jidai ni motto shikkari to benkyō shite oku beki datta yo.

I should have studied harder when I was a student.

❏ 朝ごはんをしっかり食べるのが健康の秘けつです。

Asa gohan o shikkari taberu no ga kenkō no hiketsu desu.

The secret to good health is eating a hearty breakfast.

はっきり (hakkiri) G / N

Clear, distinct; unambiguous, unmistakable.

❏ あれからもう15年もたつのに、まるできのうのことのように
はっきりと覚えているわ。

*Are kara mō jūgo-nen mo tatsu no ni, maru de kinō no koto no yō ni
hakkiri to oboete iru wa.*

That was fifteen years ago, but I still remember it all as if it were yesterday.

❏ どうもはっきりしないお天気ね。

Dōmo hakkiri shinai otenki ne.

This weather sure is fickle, isn't it.

うんざり (unzari) B

To be bored, tired, fed up. To be unwilling to endure something any
longer.

❏ いくら納豆が好きでも、毎朝毎晩納豆じゃうんざりするよ。

Ikura nattō ga suki de mo, maiasa maiban nattō ja unzari suru yo.

No matter how much you might like *nattō*, you'd get tired of it, too,
if you ate it morning and night.

❏ お説教はもううんざりよ。自分のことは自分で決めるわ。

Osekkyō wa mō unzari yo. Jibun no koto wa jibun de kimeru wa.

I'm fed up with your sermons. I'm going to live my life the way I
want to (I'll decide what's best for me).

➡ *Nattō* is made from boiled soybeans that have been fermented with a special kind
of bacteria. Due to its distinctive smell and its viscous, stringy consistency, people
either love it or hate it.

がばがば (gabagaba) N / B

(1) The sound or appearance of gurgling or gushing water (N/B).
(2) To earn or spend a lot of money (B). (3) To be baggy, too big, in reference to clothes, hats, shoes, etc. (B).

❏ 下水ががばがばいっているんだけど、どこかつまっているの
　かしら。

Gesui ga gabagaba itte iru n' da kedo, doko ka tsumatte iru no kashira.

The drainpipes have been making gurgling noises. I wonder if they're clogged up somewhere.

❏ あの会社、一時は不動産でがばがばもうかっていたらしいよ。

Ano kaisha, ichiji wa fudōsan de gabagaba mōkatte ita rashii yo.

For a while, that company was apparently raking in money hand over foot from real estate.

❏ お兄ちゃんのお下がりの靴じゃ、やっぱりがばがばね。

Onīchan no osagari no kutsu ja, yappari gabagaba ne.

Big brother's hand-me-down shoes are huge on you after all, aren't they.

がっくり (gakkuri) B

(1) To bend, fall, tip over, or collapse suddenly. By extension, to become disappointed or discouraged. (2) Used to describe a sudden loss of strength, determination, or energy, especially when the change is very great.

❏ 連れ合いが亡くなって、祖父もがっくりきたらしいんだ。

Tsureai ga naku natte, sofu mo gakkuri kita rashii n' da.

Grandfather has been down in the dumps ever since his wife died.

❏ 五十の坂を越したら、がっくり体力が落ちてね、夜ふかしが
　　まるでだめになったんだ。

*Gojū no saka o koshitara, gakkuri tairyoku ga ochite ne, yofukashi ga
maru de dame ni natta n' da.*

After hitting fifty I don't seem to have the old oomph anymore.
Staying up to all hours of the night is completely beyond me.

"PRETTY WOMAN"

Fill in the blanks with one of the words studied in this chapter: は
らはら harahara, どきどき dokidoki, ぼうっと pōtto, ぱっと／ぱ
あっと patto/pātto, うっとり uttori, しっかり shikkari, はっきり hakkiri,
うんざり unzari, がばがば gabagaba, がっくり gakkuri. There are at
least two sentences for each word. Answers are on page 220.

1 君の言動にはいつも (　　　　) させられるね。

Kimi no gendō ni wa itsumo (　　　　) saserareru ne.

Your behavior always keeps me on pins and needles.

2 ちょっと走っただけで心臓が (　　　　) いうんだから、運動
不足だね。

*Chotto hashitta dake de shinzō ga (　　　　) iu n' da kara, undō-busoku
da ne.*

After running just a little, my heart was pounding. Not enough exercise, that's for sure.

3 何を (　　　　) しているの？人の話を聞いてよ。

Nani o (　　　　) shite iru no? Hito no hanashi kiite yo.

What, are you daydreaming or something? Listen to what a person
has to say.

4 トンネルを抜けたら、目の前に (　　　　) 海の景色が広がっ
てきれいだったわ。

*Toneru o nuketara, me no mae ni (   ) umi no keshiki ga hirogatte
    kireki datta wa.*

When we came out of the tunnel, this beautiful ocean scenery sud-
    denly unfolded in front of us.

5 彼女の美しい歌声には思わず(   )と聴きほれるね。

Kanojo no utsukushii utagoe ni wa omowazu (   ) to kikihoreru ne.

Before you know it, you really fall under the spell of her beautiful
    voice.

6 包帯を(   )巻いておいてください。

Hōtai o (   ) maite oite kudasai.

Be sure that the bandages are tied tightly.

7 古いけど(   )したテーブルだから、捨てるのはもった
    いないよ。

Furui kedo (   ) shita tēburu da kara, suteru no wa mottainai yo.

It's an old table, but it's sturdy. It's a shame to throw it away.

8 何度も(   )と断ったのに、しつこいのよね。

Nando mo (   ) to kotowatta no ni, shitsukoi no yo ne.

Though I clearly turned him down a number of times, he won't take
    no for an answer.

9 2週間も入院しているともう(   )だ。

Nishū-kan mo nyūin shite iru to mō (   ) da.

After two weeks in the hospital I've had it up to here.

10 コーヒーを飲みすぎて、胃が(   )になっちゃった。

Kōhī o nomisugite, i ga (   ) ni natchatta.

I drank so much coffee that my stomach was absolutely awash with it.

11 あんなに（　　　　）お金を使えばそれは無くなるさ。

Anna ni (　　　　) okane o tsukaeba sore wa naku naru sa.

Sure, you're bound to run out of money if you throw it around like that.

12 この折れ線グラフでわかるように、昨年から売り上げが（　　　　）落ち込んでいます。

Kono oresen-gurafu de wakaru yō ni, sakunen kara uriage ga (　　　　) ochikonde imasu.

As you can see from this line graph, sales have plunged since last year.

13 お母さん、涙を（　　　　）とこぼしてかわいそうだったよ。

Okāsan, namida o (　　　　) to koboshite kawaisō datta yo.

I really felt sorry for Mother. She was shedding tears.

14 突然、前に出て挨拶しなさいなんて言われて、本当に（　　　　）したよ。

Totsuzen, mae ni dete aisatsu shinasai nante iwarete, hontō ni (　　　　) shita yo.

All of a sudden I was told, like, step forward and introduce yourself. My heart literally missed a beat.

15 顔が（　　　　）赤いけど、ビール1杯しか飲んでいないんです。

Kao ga (　　　　) akai kedo, bīru ippai shika nonde inai n' desu.

My face is flushed, but I've only had one glass of beer.

16 このところ、仕事も私生活もなんだか（　　　　）しないんだ。

Kono tokoro, shigoto mo shiseikatsu mo nan da ka (　　　　) shinai n' da.

These days, neither my work nor my private life seems to be going anywhere.

17 急に暖かくなったから、桜の花がいっぺんに（　　　　　）と開いたね。

Kyū ni atataku natta kara, sakura no hana ga ippen ni (　　　) to hiraita ne.

With the sudden warm weather, the cherry trees have bloomed all at the same time.

18 彼って（　　　　　）するようなきれいな顔立ちよね。

Kare tte (　　　) suru yō na kirei na kaodachi yo ne.

He has the kind of face that can throw a spell over you.

19 （　　　　　）した息子さんがいらして、うらやましいわ。

(　　　) shita musuko-san ga irashite, urayamashii wa.

I envy you for having such a reliable son.

20 今のうちに（　　　　　）貯金をしておいたほうがいいよ。

Ima no uchi ni (　　　) chokin o shite oita hō ga ii yo.

You had better start seriously saving now, while there's still time.

21 彼の話はいつも要点が（　　　　　）しないわね。

Kare no hanashi wa itsumo yōten ga (　　　) shinai wa ne.

It's never quite clear what the point is when he's talking.

22 （　　　　　）するほど、愚痴を聞かされました。

(　　　) suru hodo, guchi o kikasaremashita.

I had to listen to so much griping that I really got fed up.

23 10キロやせたら、洋服が全部（　　　　　）で着られなくなっちゃった。

Jukkiro yasetara, yōfuku ga zenbu (   ) *de kirarenaku natchatta.*

I lost ten kilos, and all my clothes got so baggy that I couldn't wear them.

24 そんなに（   ）しないで。いいこともあるよ。

Sonna ni (   ) *shinai de. Ii koto mo aru yo.*

Don't take it so hard. Something good is bound to happen.

A ROMANTIC FLAIR

Tomoko Tabuchi wants a change of mood, so she has come to the beauty parlor to have her hair done in a different style. She hopes to look more feminine, to have more of a romantic flair. The hairdresser is Seiichi Nishi.

田淵　「秋だから、**ふわっと**ロマンチックな頭にしたいんだけど。」

西　　「お客様のおぐし*は、細くて**さらさら**なので、ストレート
　　　も悪くないと思いますけどね。」

田淵　「それがいやなのよ。雨が降ると、**ぺしゃんこ**になっちゃ
　　　うし。何だか†子供っぽい感じがして。」

西　　「そうですか。もったいないですね。**ごわごわ**していやだ
　　　とおっしゃるお客様も多いのに。」

田淵　「そうかしら。寝癖はついて**ぼさぼさ**になるし、頭の形の
　　　悪さは**くっきり**出ちゃうし、いやだわ。」

西　　「それじゃ、**ふんわり**全体にパーマをかけますか。そうす
　　　れば、**ぺたんと**なることはないでしょう。」

田淵　「でも、**ちりちり**にだけはならないようにしてよ。」

西　　「おまかせください。ロマンチックに**ばっちり**決めてみせ
　　　ますよ。ただし、あとはお客様次第ですけどね。」

❈ *Ogushi*: hair; a polite term used largely by woman.
† *Nan da ka*: something, somehow, sort of.

Tabuchi: *Aki da kara, fuwatto romanchikku na atama ni shitai n' da kedo.*

Nishi: *Okyaku-sama no ogushi wa, hosokute sarasara na no de, sutorēto mo waruku nai to omoimasu kedo ne.*

Tabuchi: *Sore ga iya na no yo. Ame ga furu to, peshanko ni natchau shi. Nan da ka kodomo-ppoi kanji ga shite.*

Nishi: *Sō desu ka. Mottai-nai desu ne. Gowagowa shite iya da to ossharu okyaku-sama mo ōi no ni.*

Tabuchi: *Sō kashira. Neguse wa tsuite bosabosa ni naru shi, atama no katachi no warusa wa kukkiri dechau shi, iya da wa.*

Nishi: *Sore ja, funwari zentai ni pāma o kakemasu ka. Sō sureba, petanto naru koto wa nai deshō.*

Tabuchi: *Demo, chirichiri ni dake wa naranai yō ni shite yo.*

Nishi: *Omakase kudasai. Romanchikku ni batchiri kimete misemasu yo. Tadashi, ato wa okyaku-sama–shidai desu kedo ne.*

✻ ✻ ✻

Tabuchi: It's autumn, so I'd like my hair to look softer, lighter, more romantic.

Nishi: Your hair is very fine and silky. It wouldn't look bad if you just left it straight, you know.

Tabuchi: That's exactly what I don't like about it. When it rains, it loses all its fluff. And besides, it makes me look like a little girl somehow…

Nishi: Really? That's a shame. Many of our customers complain about their hair being hard and stiff.

Tabuchi: Well, maybe that's okay for them. I don't like silky hair because it gets all messed up when I sleep on it. It shows the lousy shape of my head, too.

Nishi:	Okay, then. How about a fluffy, all-over perm? That way it won't go flat on you.
Tabuchi:	But just make sure it doesn't get all frizzy.
Nishi:	Trust me. When you leave here, you'll definitely look romantic. After that, it's all up to you.

ふわっと (fuwatto)　G / N

Soft and light. Downy, puffy, feathery. Used to describe something that is moving or floating gently.

❏ あのふわっとした雲、まるで綿菓子みたいだね。

Ano fuwatto shita kumo, maru de wata-gashi mitai da ne.

Those fluffy clouds look just like cotton candy.

❏ あのマジック・ショーにはびっくりしたわ、横になっていた人がふわっと浮くんですもの。

Ano majikku-shō ni wa bikkuri shita wa, yoko ni natte ita hito ga fuwatto uku n' desu mono.

I was really astonished by that magic show. The man lying on his back actually floated right up into the air.

さらさら (sarasara)　G / N

Smooth, dry, clean, not sticky or damp (G). Used to describe the sound or feel of light, silky hair or fabric rubbing together gently (G/N). *Sarasara* can also express the smooth feeling of water flowing in a shallow brook or the fluency of a speaker or writer (G).

❏ 今日は天気がよかったから、洗濯物がさらさらに乾いたわ。

Kyō wa tenki ga yokatta kara, sentaku-mono ga sarasara ni kawaita wa.

It was nice weather today, so the laundry that was put out to dry got good and fluffy.

❏ 飲んだ後のお茶漬けさらさら、これがうまいんだなあ。

Nonda ato no ochazuke sarasara, kore ga umai n' da nā.

After a few drinks, there is nothing nicer than the way a bowl of tea and rice slides smoothly down the throat.

❏ 小川がさらさら流れている風景なんて、もう何年も見たことがないなあ。

Ogawa ga sarasara nagarete iru fūkei nante, mō nan-nen mo mita koto ga nai nā.

It seems like years since I last saw a landscape with a gently flowing stream.

❏ 朝青龍にサインを頼んだら、いやがらずにさらさらと書いてくれたわ。

Asashōryū ni sain o tanondara, iyagarazu ni sarasara to kaite kureta wa.

When I asked the sumo wrestler Asashōryū for his autograph, he dashed one off without the slightest fuss.

➥ *Chazuke* (茶漬け) refers to Japanese tea or a thin broth poured over white rice. It can be elaborate. *Tai chazuke* (鯛茶漬け) and *sake chazuke* (鮭茶漬け), for example, include pieces of sea bream and salmon, respectively. Or it can be simple with just some pickles or a little garnish scattered on top of cold, leftover rice. The usual image of *chazuke*, however, is of a plain meal that is easy to prepare. The combination of rice with tea or broth makes for easy eating, so it is a good light meal after you've had a few drinks or on other occasions. *Chazuke* is held in such high regard that it is usually sports the honorific *o*: *ochazuke*.

ぺしゃんこ／ぺちゃんこ (peshanko/pechanko) N / B

Flattened, pressed down, crushed. By extension, *peshanko* and *pe-chanko* can also express defeat or complete failure.

❑ 鼻ぺちゃだなんて失礼ね、私の鼻はそんなにぺちゃんこ
　じゃないわ。

Hana-pecha da nante shitsurei ne, watashi no hana wa sonna ni pechanko ja nai wa.

My nose is flat as a pancake, you say? How insulting can you get! It's not that flat at all.

❑ きのうの会議は散々だったよ、反対派にぺしゃんこにやら
　れちゃってね。

Kinō no kaigi wa sanzan datta yo, hantai-ha ni peshanko ni yarare-chatte ne.

Yesterday's meeting was terrible. I was raked over the coals by the opposition.

ごわごわ (gowagowa) N / B

Stiff, rigid. Used to describe paper, cloth, leather, etc.

❑ このシーツ、糊がききすぎてごわごわになっちゃったわ。

Kono shītsu, nori ga kikisugite gowagowa ni natchatta wa.

These sheets have too much starch. They're stiff as a board.

❑ 旅館の浴衣ってどこでもごわごわだね。

Ryokan no yukata tte doko de mo gowagowa da ne.

No matter what Japanese inn you go to, the *yukata* are as stiff as cardboard.

➥ A single-layer kimono made of cotton is called a 浴衣 *yukata* (the word *kimono* refers nowadays to a silk garment worn principally on formal occasions). Originally made of linen and worn by samurai and the nobility as a kind of bathrobe, *yukata* dyed with simple indigo-and-white patterns later spread among the common people. Now they are popular during the hot summer months and as cool robes after hot baths. *Yukata*-clad women and children lend a colorful air to *Obon* dancing and other summer festivals. Japanese inns—*ryokan*—provide *yukata* to their guests both for sleeping and lounging. While their uniform size is convenient, the *yukata* at Japanese inns are invariably stiff and starchy.

ぼさぼさ (bosabosa) B

(1) Tussled, tangled, uncombed; used to describe not only hair but also brushes, brooms, and similar objects. (2) To sit around vacantly, not doing what needs to be done.

❑ そんなぼさぼさ頭じゃ女の子にもてない*わよ。

Sonna bosabosa-atama ja onna no ko ni motenai wa yo.

You'll never get any girlfriends with your hair looking like a haystack.

> ❊ *Moteru*: to be popular, especially with the opposite sex.

❑ 君、ぼさぼさしていないで手伝ったらどうだ。

Kimi, bosabosa shite inai de tetsudattara dō da.

How about giving me a hand instead of sitting around like a bump on a log?

くっきり (kukkiri) G / N

Distinct, clearly visible.

❑ 見晴らしがいいわね。富士山がくっきり見えるわ。

Miharashi ga ii wa ne. Fuji-san ga kukkiri mieru wa.

What a wonderful view! You can see Mt. Fuji as plain as day.

❏ 夜になると、東京タワーがくっきりと浮かび上がってきれいだよ。

Yoru ni naru to, Tōkyō-tawā ga kukkiri to ukabiagatte kirei da yo.

Tokyo Tower is really pretty at night, the way it rises up into the air so sharp and clear.

➡ Located in Shiba Kōen, a couple of miles south of the Imperial Palace, Tokyo Tower has observation platforms as well as broadcasting antennas for several television stations. After its completion in 1958, it came to symbolize Tokyo's postwar modernization, the television age, and the 1964 Tokyo Olympics. You may have seen it destroyed more than once by prehistoric beasts in Japanese monster films of the 1960s. Modeled on the Eiffel Tower (though about 110 feet taller), Tokyo Tower is nondescript by day, but when lit up at night the tower becomes a distinctive landmark visible throughout the city.

ふんわり／ふわり (funwari/fuwari) G / N

Gently swelling, floating, billowing. Used to describe the motion of soft, light objects floating in the air (parachutes, birds, etc.) or gently covering other objects (sheets, quilts, etc.). *Fuwatto* (the first word in this list) emphasizes the floating or rising motion, while *funwari* and *fuwari* suggest a gentler feeling. Of these latter two, *funwari* implies lighter and calmer motions.

❏ 布団を干したから、ふんわりして気持ちよくなったわよ。

Futon o hoshita kara, funwari shite kimochi yoku natta wa yo.

I hung the futons out in the sun, so now they feel nice and fluffy.

❏ 丹頂鶴がふわりと雪の中に舞い上がるのを見ていると、きれいで見飽きないよ。

Tanchō-zuru ga fuwari to yuki no naka ni maiagaru no o mite iru to, kirei de miakinai yo.

The sight of white cranes soaring up into the falling snow is so beautiful that you never grow tired of it.

❏ 美奈子さん、淡いピンクのセーターに絹のスカーフをふわりと巻いて、春らしい装いだったわ。

Minako-san, awai pinku no sētā ni kinu no sukāfu o fuwari to maite, haru-rashii yosōi datta wa.

With a silk scarf wrapped lightly around her neck and a pale pink sweater, Minako had a very springtime look.

ぺたんと (petanto) N / B

Flat, smooth, level (N). Also used to describe the sound or action of pressing a label, sticker, or other object onto a flat surface (N). Another meaning is to flop onto the floor in a slovenly manner (N/B).

❏ 私、ハイヒールは苦手なの。いつもぺたんとした底の靴をはいているわ。

Watashi, haihīru wa nigate na no. Itsumo petan to shita soko no kutsu o haite iru wa.

I'm just no good with high heels. That's why I always wear flats.

❏ 運転の方はどうかなあ。彼の車には初心者マークがぺたんとはってあったもの。

Unten no hō wa dō ka nā. Kare no kuruma ni wa shoshin-sha–māku ga petan to hatte atta mono.

I'm not so sure about his driving. His car has a beginner's sticker plastered on it.

❏ あんまり驚いたので、ぺたんと尻もちをついちゃったわ。

Anmari odoroita no de, petan to shirimochi o tsuichatta wa.

I was so startled I fell flat on my rear end.

ちりちり (chirichiri) N / B

Curly, frizzy. Used especially to describe hair, yarn, etc. that has been scorched and shriveled (N). Can also express tingling caused by extreme heat or shivering caused by cold or fear (N/B).

❏ 小さいときには、ちりちりの頭をずいぶん気にしてたのよ。

Chiisai toki ni wa, chirichiri no atama o zuibun ki ni shite 'ta no yo.

When I was small, I used to worry a lot about my frizzy hair.

❏ ちりちりと何か焦げるにおいがするけれど、大丈夫かしら。

Chirichiri to nani ka kogeru nioi ga suru keredo, daijōbu kashira.

It smells like something's gotten scorched. I wonder if everything's all right.

❏ 風呂といえば家内は熱いのが好きでしてね、肌がちりちり
　するようなお湯に平気で入るんですよ。

Furo to ieba kanai wa atsui no ga suki deshite ne, hada ga chirichiri suru yō na oyu ni heiki de hairu n' desu yo.

Talking about baths, my wife likes them really hot, you see. She thinks nothing of getting into a scalding tub.

➡ Japanese baths have two parts, the tub itself (called the 湯舟 *yubune*) and a washing area (洗い場 *araiba*). Whether at a private home or a public bath, proper etti-quette dictates you should first rinse off your body in the washing area before entering the tub, since other people will be using the same water later. Then you can relax in the tub with the hot water up to your neck, soap yourself up and rinse off again in the washing area, and then get back in the tub for a final soak. These days, most bathtubs in Japan are made of stainless steel, porcelain, plastic, or tile, but the traditional wooden baths made of cedar are still prized for their subtle aroma.

ばっちり (batchiri) G

Precise, accurate, just right. Good, well done. Used informally.

❏ 原さんはいつも頭のてっぺんからつま先までばっちり決め
ています*ね。

Hara-san wa itsumo atama no teppen kara tsumasaki made batchiri kimete imasu ne.

Mr. Hara is always dressed just so, from head to foot.

❋ *Kimeru*: to dress properly.

❏ あんちょこがあるから、試験はばっちりよ。

Anchoko ga aru kara, shiken wa batchiri yo.

I have the answer book, so I'm gonna ace the test.

Quiz

Fill in the blanks with one of the words studied in this chapter: ふわっと fuwatto, さらさら sarasara, ぺしゃんこ／ぺちゃんこ peshanko/pechanko, ごわごわ gowagowa, ぼさぼさ bosabosa, くっきり kukkiri, ふんわり／ふわり funwari/fuwari, ぺたんと petanto, ちりちり chirichiri, ばっちり batchiri. There are at least two sentences for each word. Answers are on page 220.

1 気球が（　　　　　）浮いたときには感動しました。

Kikyū ga (　　　　　) uita toki ni wa kandō shimashita.

When the (hot-air) balloon floated lightly up, I really felt moved.

2 雪にも（　　　　　）の雪と、湿った雪とがあるよね。

Yuki ni mo (　　　　　) no yuki to, shimetta yuki to ga aru yo ne.

Even with snow, there's fine, powdery snow and there's moist snow.

3 生徒にあんなに言い負かされたら、先生のプライドも（　　　　　）だね。

Seito ni anna ni iimakasaretara, sensei no puraido mo (　　　　　) da ne.

If you lose an argument to a student like that, a teacher's pride is bound to be deflated.

4 このタオル、（　　　　　）で顔を拭くと痛いよ。

Kono taoru, (　　　　　) de kao o fuku to itai yo.

This towel is so rough, if you dry your face with it, it actually hurts.

5 髪<ruby>かみ</ruby>をとかしたほうがいいわよ。（　　　）だから。

Kami o tokashita hō ga ii wa yo. (　　　) da kara.

You'd better comb your hair. It's a mess.

6 夕日<ruby>ゆうひ</ruby>の中<ruby>なか</ruby>に木々<ruby>きぎ</ruby>の輪郭<ruby>りんかく</ruby>が（　　　）と浮<ruby>う</ruby>かび上<ruby>あ</ruby>がって、きれいだったわ。

Yūhi no naka ni kigi no rinkaku ga (　　　) to ukabiagatte, kirei datta wa.

The trees were silhouetted against the sunset. It was really lovely.

7 宇宙飛行士<ruby>うちゅうひこうし</ruby>が（　　　）と船内<ruby>せんない</ruby>に漂<ruby>ただよ</ruby>っている映像<ruby>えいぞう</ruby>がテレビに映<ruby>うつ</ruby>った。

Uchū-hikōshi ga (　　　) to sennai ni tadayotte iru eizō ga terebi ni utsutta.

The television showed the image of astronauts floating inside the shuttle.

8 山道<ruby>やまみち</ruby>で滑<ruby>すべ</ruby>って（　　　）しりもちをついちゃったんだ。

Yamamichi de subette (　　　) shirimochi o tsuichatta n' da.

I slipped on the mountain path and fell flat on my butt.

9 （　　　）という音<ruby>おと</ruby>がしたら、焦<ruby>こ</ruby>げないように火<ruby>ひ</ruby>を細<ruby>ほそ</ruby>めてください。

(　　　) to iu oto ga shitara, kogenai yō ni hi o hosomete kudasai.

If you hear a sizzling sound, please turn down the flame so it doesn't get burnt.

10 今日のスピーチは（　　　　）決めようね。

Kyō no supīchi wa (　　　) kemeyō ne.

Let's make today's speech right on the money, okay.

11 羽毛の枕は（　　　）としていて、気持ちがいいね。

Umō no makura wa (　　　) to shite ite, kimochi ga ii ne.

Down pillows are so fluffy, they really feel great.

12 彼女のまっすぐで（　　　）した髪、きれいね。

Kanojo no massugu de (　　　) shita kami, kirei ne.

Her straight, satiny hair is really beautiful.

13 せっかくケーキを買ってきたのに、込んだ電車で（　　　　）になっちゃったよ。

Sekkaku kēki o katte kita no ni, konda densha de (　　　　) ni natchatta yo.

Here I'd bought some cake, but it got squashed flat on the crowded train.

14 鼻をかみすぎて、鼻の周りの皮膚が（　　　　）になっちゃった。

Hana o kamisugite, hana no mawari no hifu ga (　　　　) ni natchatta.

I blew my nose so much that the skin has become all dry and hard.

15 東京は人が多いから、（　　　）してたら、歩けないよ。

Tōkyō wa hito ga ōi kara, (　　　) shite 'tara, arukenai yo.

There are so many people in Tokyo that you can't take a walk without keeping your wits about you.

16 天気がよかったから、遠くの島が（　　　）見えた。

Tenki ga yokatta kara, tōku no shima ga (   ) mieta.

The weather was so good I could clearly see an island off in the distance.

17 綿のような雲が青空に（　　　　）浮いている。

Wata no yō na aozora ni (   ) uite iru.

A cottony cloud was floating in the clear blue sky.

18 そのくらいの腰痛なら、このシップ薬を（　　　　）はっておけば治るよ。

Sono kurai no yōtsū nara, kono shippu-yaku o (   ) hatte okeba naoru yo.

For a backache like that, you can fix it by simply slapping on this compress.

19 パーマをかけたら（　　　　）になっちゃって、恥ずかしいわ。

Pāma o kaketara (   ) ni natchatte, hazukashii wa.

I got a permanent, and it came out frizzy. How embarrassing!

20 昨日（　　　　）ボーナスをもらったから、ご飯をご馳走するよ。

Kinō (   ) bōnasu o moratta kara, gohan o gochisō suru yo.

Yesterday I had the pleasure of getting my bonus, so I'll take you out to eat.

THE RUSH HOUR

Yoshio Watanabe and Kazuhiko Tanaka work at the Shinjuku Life Insurance Company. One morning in early summer, they happen to run into each other on a commuter train.

渡辺　　（電車に乗ろうとして）「あ、おはようございます、田中さん。」

田中　　「おはようございます。」
　　　　（ドアが閉まりかけて駅員に押される）

渡辺　　「うわっ、いてててて＊。」
　　　　（ドアが閉まって）

渡辺　　「毎日これだからいやですね。**ぎゅうぎゅう**詰めの電車
　　　　で、汗を**だらだら**かきながら通勤ですから。」

田中　　「まったくです。会社に着くころには**くたくた**ですよ。」

渡辺　　「ワイシャツも**べとべと**になるしね。」
　　　　（カップルで通勤している男女を見て）

田中　　「朝から**べったり**くっついているカップルもはた迷惑†だ
　　　　よね。」

渡辺　　「ほんと＊。いちゃいちゃ＊**べたべた**しちゃって。」

田中　　「**こそこそ**話したり、**くすくす**笑ったり。まったくもう。＊」

渡辺　　「**ちゃらちゃら**している女も女だけど、**でれでれ**している
　　　　男も男だよ。」

田中　　「**いらいら**しますよね。」
　　　　（電車が大きく揺れて、カップルの顔が見える）

石田　　「あっ、渡辺さんおはようございます。」

渡辺　　「あれっ。石田さんじゃないですか。」

石田　　「家内です。」

渡辺　　「うらやましいですなあ。朝から若くてきれいな奥さん
　　　　と出勤なんて。」

✿ *Itetete*: from *itai*, "it hurts."

† *Hata-meiwaku*: annoying to others nearby.

❖ *Honto*: colloquial contraction of *hontō*.

❖ For *ichaicha*: see "A Spat" (p. 143).

❊ *Mattaku mō*: abbreviation of something like *Mattaku mō iya ni natchau yo ne* (roughly, "I'm absolutely tired of this already").

Watanabe: *(Densha ni norō to shite)* A, *ohayō gozaimasu, Tanaka-san.*

Tanaka: *Ohayō gozaimasu.*
(Doa ga shimarikakete eki-in ni osareru)

Watanabe: *Uwa—, itetetete.*
(Doa ga shimatte)

Watanabe: *Mainichi kore da kara iya desu ne. Gyūgyū-zume no den-sha de, ase o daradara kakinagara tsūkin desu kara.*

Tanaka: *Mattaku desu. Kaisha ni tsuku koro ni wa kutakuta desu yo.*

Watanabe: *Waishatsu mo betobeto ni naru shi ne.*
(Kappuru de tsūkin shite iru danjo o mite)

Tanaka: *Asa kara bettari kuttsuite iru kappuru mo hata-meiwaku da yo ne.*

Watanabe: *Honto. Ichaicha betabeta shichatte.*

Tanaka: *Kosokoso hanashitari, kusukusu warattari. Mattaku mō.*

Watanabe: *Charachara shite iru onna mo onna da kedo, deredere shite iru otoko mo otoko da yo.*

Tanaka: *Iraira shimasu yo ne. (Densha ga ōkiku yurete, kappuru no kao ga mieru)*

Ishida: *A—, Watanabe-san ohayō gozaimasu.*

Watanabe: *Are—. Ishida-san ja nai desu ka.*

Ishida: *Kanai desu.*

Watanabe: *Urayamashii desu nā. Asa kara wakakute kirei na okusan to shukkin nante.*

✷ ✷ ✷

Watanabe: (about to board the train) Ah, Tanaka. Good morning.

Tanaka: Good morning.

Watanabe: (shoved in by a station attendant as the door closes) Yipes! Ouch ouch ouch!!!

Watanabe: (after the door has closed) This is why I hate commuting every day. Packed into a train like a bunch of sardines, we get drenched in sweat just getting to work.

Tanaka: You can say that again. By the time you get to the office, you're absolutely beat.

Watanabe: And your shirt gets all sticky, besides.
(Here they notice a young couple.)

Tanaka: They're a real eyesore, aren't they, these young couples hanging all over each other first thing in the morning.

Watanabe: And how! They're so kissy-kissy, lovey-dovey.

Tanaka: Whispering to each other, giggling… It's just too much! (Give me a break!)

Watanabe: I don't know which is worse: the girl flirting with the guy or the guy making goo-goo eyes at the girl.

Tanaka: It's downright annoying, isn't it.
(The train lurches, and the couple's faces come into view.)

Ishida: Ah, Watanabe. Good morning.

Watanabe: Why, if it isn't Ishida.

Ishida: And this is my wife.

Watanabe: How lucky can you be, on your way to work with such a pretty young wife…

ぎゅうぎゅう (gyūgyū) N / B

(1) To push, pull, twist, press, jam, or squeeze completely, leaving no leeway or slack. (2) To pester, harass, torment, or—as in the second example—train someone rigorously and without mercy.

❏ 太っちゃって困るわ。ジーパンのジッパー、ぎゅうぎゅう引っぱらないと上がらないのよ。

Futotchatte komaru wa. Jīpan no jippā, gyūgyū hipparanai to agaranai no yo.

My gosh, I've put on so much weight I can't get the zipper up on my jeans unless I really yank on it.

❏ 学生時代には水泳部でね、コーチにぎゅうぎゅう絞られたよ。

Gakusei-jidai ni wa suiei-bu de ne, kōchi ni gyūgyū shiborareta yo.

When I was on the swim team in college, the coach really put us through the wringer.

➥ Rush hour around Tokyo and other big Japanese cities is a wonder to behold. Nearly everyone travels by train or subway, and one-way commutes of more than an hour are typical. At the busiest times—between 7 and 9 A.M. and 6 and 8 P.M.—trains on some lines run less than two minutes apart. Nevertheless, they get so crowded that attendants at some stations have to push the overflowing passengers onto the train so the doors can close. The worst times are the summer, when even air-conditioned coaches get hot and sticky, and the winter, when people's bulky coats make the crush even tighter.

だらだら (daradara)　N / B

(1) The continuous dripping of sweat, blood, saliva, or another thickish liquid (N). (2) To drag on, to continue without a reasonable conclusion; to dawdle, to loaf (B). (3) Used to describe a gentle slope (N).

❏ エアロビクスを1時間もやれば、汗がだらだら流れるわよ。

Earobikusu o ichi-jikan mo yareba, ase ga daradara nagareru wa yo.

After doing aerobics for an hour, I'm simply dripping with sweat.

❏ 血がだらだら流れるような番組を見ながら、よく*ご飯が食べられるわね。

Chi ga daradara nagareru yō na bangumi o minagara, yoku gohan ga taberareru wa ne.

It's amazing how you can eat while watching such a gory program.

> ❊ *Yoku*: ironical usage, hinting at the audacity, impertinence, or nerve shown in carrying out an action.

❏ だらだら残業をしていればいいっていうもんじゃないんだよ、君。

Daradara zangyō o shite ireba ii tte iu mon ja nai n' da yo, kimi.

Listen, my friend. Overtime is not just a matter of whiling the hours away.

❏ 郵便局の手前を右に入って、だらだらした坂を上りきるとうちなの。よかったらいらして。

Yūbin-kyoku no temae o migi ni haitte, daradara shita saka o agarikiru to uchi na no. Yokattara irashite.

If you turn right just before the post office and then go all the way up the gradual slope, there's my house. Feel free to drop by.

くたくた (kutakuta) N / B

(1) Tired, exhausted, worn out, beat. (2) Limp, withered, collapsed, unable to maintain the proper shape.

❏ きょうは一日中引っ越しの手伝いをしたから、くたくただよ。

Kyō wa ichinichi-jū hikkoshi no tetsudai o shita kara, kutakuta da yo.

I spent all day helping someone move, so now I'm totally wiped out.

❏ おひたし*はくたくたになるまで煮ちゃだめよ。

Ohitashi wa kutakuta ni naru made nicha dame yo.

When you boil *ohitashi*, don't let it get all soft and limp.

> ❈ *Ohitashi*: lightly boiled greens flavored with soy sauce and covered with flakes of dried bonito; typical Japanese home cooking.

べとべと (betobeto) N / B

Sticky, pasty, gluey, gummy, viscous.

❏ べとべとのガムを髪の毛にくっつけるなんて、悪質ないたずらね。

Betobeto no gamu o kami no ke ni kuttsukeru nante, akushitsu na itazura ne.

That's a pretty awful prank, putting sticky chewing gum into somebody's hair.

❏ ヘア・クリームはべとべとしているから、あんまり好きじゃないんだ。

Hea-kurīmu wa betobeto shite iru kara, anmari suki ja nai n' da.

I'm not very partial to hair oil because it's so sticky.

べったり (bettari) N / B

(1) Used to describe a sticky or adhesive object that is attached firmly to another object (N). (2) By extension, it can also refer to two people who are very close or intimate, especially when one person is overly dependent. Both meanings emphasize that the connection or relationship continues for some time (N/B).

❏ コートに泥がべったり付いているけど、一体どうしたの。

Kōto ni doro ga bettari tsuite iru kedo, ittai dō shita no.

Your coat is plastered with mud. How on earth did that happen?

❏ 大学生になっても母親べったりの息子なんて、気持ち悪いよ。

Daigaku-sei ni natte mo haha-oya–bettari no musuko nante, kimochi warui yo.

It's pretty sickening to see a guy already in college who hangs on his mother like that.

べたべた (betabeta) B

(1) Sticky, gummy. (2) Used to describe a man and woman who are overtly and immoderately affectionate. (3) For a great many pieces of paper (posters, fliers, etc.) to be pasted on a surface, for a paper to be stamped with many seals, for a surface to be covered too thickly with paint, etc. Excess is emphasized. While *betobeto* focuses on the stickiness of an object in itself, *betabeta* emphasizes the fact that one object sticks to another. Thus *betobeto* would not be possible for meanings (2) and (3).

❏ 汗っかき*ですぐ手がべたべたするの、いやになるわ。

Asekkaki de sugu te ga betabeta suru no, iya ni naru wa.

I sweat a lot, so my hands get sticky right away. It's so annoying.

    ✤ *Asekkaki*: colloquial for *asekaki*, or someone who sweats a great deal.

❏ 町中であんまりカップルにべたべたされると、夏なんか暑苦しいよね。

Machinaka de anmari kappuru ni betabeta sareru to, natsu nanka atsukurushii yo ne.

When you see young couples around town hanging all over each other, summer seems hotter than ever.

❏ うちの塀に無断でポスターをべたべたはられちゃって、はがすのに一苦労だったよ。

Uchi no hei ni mudan de posutā o betabeta hararechatte, hagasu no ni hito-kurō datta yo.

Somebody stuck a bunch of posters all over our wall without permission. It was a tough job getting them off.

こそこそ (kosokoso) B

Secretive, sneaky, furtive, sly.

❏ こそこそと人の悪口を言うなんて最低だよ。

Kosokoso to hito no warukuchi o iu nante saitei da yo.

Nothing's worse than bad-mouthing somebody behind their back.

❏ うちの子ったら、ちょっと目を離すとこそこそいたずらしているんだから困るわ。

Uchi no ko ttara, chotto me o hanasu to kosokoso itazura shite iru n' da kara komaru wa.

If I take my eyes off my son for even a second, he sneaks off and gets into some mischief. It's a real problem.

くすくす (kusukusu) N / B

To giggle or titter, especially in a suppressed voice. Usually used to describe women.

❑ どうも人がくすくす笑うと思ったら、洗濯屋の名札をつけたまま背広を着てたんだ。

Dōmo hito ga kusukusu warau to omottara, sentaku-ya no nafuda o tsuketa mama sebiro o kite 'ta n' da.

I had this feeling people were laughing behind my back, and sure enough, the suit I was wearing still had the dry-cleaner's tag on it.

❑ お葬式でくすくす笑うなんて不謹慎だよ。

Osōshiki de kusukusu warau nante fu-kinshin da yo.

It's discourteous to giggle like that at a funeral.

ちゃらちゃら (charachara) N / B

(1) Rattle, jangle, clatter. The sound of small, thin metallic objects striking against each other or against something hard (N). (2) Flirtatious, coquettish, fawning. Also used to criticize the wearing of flashy, gaudy clothes. Principally used to describe women who flirt and fawn. When describing a man, the word suggests effeminacy (B).

❑ 小銭をズボンのポケットに入れておくと、ちゃらちゃらいってみっともないわよ。

Kozeni o zubon no poketto ni irete oku to, charachara itte mittomo-nai wa yo.

You're going to seem pretty silly if you put a lot of jangling coins in your pocket.

❑ 彼女ったら、ちゃらちゃらしちゃって、会社を何だと思ってい
るのかしら。

Kanojo ttara, charachara shichatte, kaisha o nan da to omotte iru no kashira.

She's really something, decked out fit to kill and playing up to (flirting with) every guy in the office. Where does she think she is, anyway?

でれでれ (deredere) B

(1) Sloppy, undisciplined, loose, slovenly. (2) *Deredere* is often used to describe a man who fawns upon a woman in a disgraceful or unbecoming manner.

❑ 道いっぱいに広がってしゃべりながらでれでれ歩いている
人たちって、本当に迷惑よね。

Michi iipai ni hirogatte shaberinagara deredere aruite iru hitotachi tte, hontō ni meiwaku yo ne.

People who blithely stroll along chattering among themselves and blocking the street are really a nuisance.

❑ 女の子に囲まれるとすぐでれでれするんだから、課長も
困ったもんだよ。

Onna no ko ni kakomareru to sugu deredere suru n' da kara, kachō mo komatta mon da yo.

The section chief is really a case, the way he gets all goofy-eyed whenever he's surrounded by the office girls.

いらいら (iraira) B

To become irritated, annoyed, or fidgety because things do not work out as expected. The word may refer to one's facial expression, actions, or manner of speaking. It is derived from the older *ira* ("thorn"). (During the Iran-Iraq War of the 1980s, some clever headline writers called it the イライラ戦争 *ira-ira sensō*, abbreviating the names of the two countries to express irritation about the interminable conflict.)

❑ 公衆電話で長話をされるといらいらするね。

Kōshū-denwa de nagabanashi o sareru to iraira suru ne.

I get antsy if I have to wait while somebody talks for a long time on a pay phone.

❑ 高速道路の渋滞ほどいらいらするものはないわね。

Kōsoku-dōro no jūtai hodo iraira suru mono wa nai wa ne.

Nothing sets your nerves more on edge than being caught in traffic on the expressway.

The Rush Hour

Fill in the blanks with one of the words studied in this chapter: ぎゅうぎゅう gyūgyū, だらだら daradara, くたくた kutakuta, べとべと betobeto, べったり bettari, べたべた betabeta, こそこそ kosokoso, くすくす kusukusu, ちゃらちゃら charachara, でれでれ deredere, いらいら iraira. There are at least two sentences for each word. Answers are on page 221.

■1 雑巾は（　　　　　）よく絞ってください。

Zōkin wa (　　　　　) yoku shibotte kudasai.

Please give the cleaning rags a good wringing out.

■2 赤ん坊が（　　　　　）よだれをたらしているのは健康な証拠だよ。

Akanbō ga (　　　　　) yodare o tarashite iru no wa kenkō na shōko da yo.

The fact that the baby is drooling is a sign that it is healthy.

■3 慣れない仕事だったので（　　　　　）になった。

Narenai shigoto datta no de (　　　　　) ni natta.

It was unfamiliar work, and it completely wore me out.

■4 （　　　　　）のペンキが手についちゃった。

(　　　　　) no penki ga te ni tsuichatta.

I got this sticky paint on my hands.

5 二人はまだ新婚だから（　　　　　）だよ。

Futari wa mada shinkon da kara (　　　　) da yo.

They're still newlyweds, so they're pretty much all over each other.

6 タイヤに（　　　　　）くっついた泥がなかなかとれないんだ。

Taiya ni (　　　　) kuttsuite ita doro ga nakanaka torenai n' da.

It's really hard to get off the mud that's plastered to the tires.

7 （　　　　　）と陰で話していないで、堂々とおっしゃったらいかがですか。

(　　　　) to kage de hanashite inai de, dōdō to osshattara ikaga desu ka.

How would it be if you told me straight out and stopped whispering behind my back.

8 真面目な話をしているのに（　　　　　）笑うのは失礼です。

Majime na hanashi o shite iru no ni (　　　) warau no wa shitsurei desu.

It's rude to snicker while I'm talking about something serious.

9 そんな（　　　　　）した格好で出勤するな。

Sonna (　　　　) shita kakkō de shukkin suru na.

Don't go to work all decked out like that.

10 彼は15才も若い奥さんと結婚したから、いつも（　　　　　）しています。

Kare wa jūgo-sai mo wakai okusan to kekkon shita kara, itsumo (　　　) shite imasu.

Since his new wife is fifteen years younger, he's always fawning over her.

11 そんなに（　　　　　）しながら運転すると危ないですよ。

Sonna ni (   ) *shinagara unten suru to abunai desu yo.*

It's unsafe to be driving while you're feeling so edgy.

12 野 球 部で(   )にしごかれて、よく泣いて帰ってきたもんだよ。

Yakyū-bu de (   ) *ni shigokarete, yoku naite kaette kita mon da yo.*

On the baseball team we were put through the wringer, and I often cried my way home.

13 語学は(   )勉 強 したのでは、効果は出ないよ。

Gogaku wa (   ) *benkyō shita no de wa, kōka wa denai yo.*

With languages, you won't get good results by studying in a leisurely fashion.

14 (   )としたなだらかな坂を下ると、駅前の交差点に出るんだ。

(   ) *to shita nadaraka na saka o kudaru to, ekimae no kōsaten ni deru n' da.*

You go down this gentle slope and you come out at the crossing in front of the station.

15 このコート、15年も着ているのでもう(   )だ。

Kono kōto, jūgo-nen mo kite iru no de mō (   ) *da.*

I've been wearing this coat for fifteen years, and it's pretty shapeless now.

16 テーブルの上に蜂蜜がこぼれて(   )だわ。

Tēburu no ue ni hachimitsu ga koborete (   ) *da wa.*

Honey got spilt on the table and it's all sticky.

17 息子の部屋の壁には(   )と彼女の写真が貼ってある。

Musuko no heya no kabe ni wa (   ) to kanojo no shashin ga hatte aru.

On the wall of my son's room his girlfriend's pictures are plastered here and there.

18 彼女は何から何まで（   ）彼に頼っているね。

Kanojo wa nani kara nani made (   ) kare ni tayotte iru ne.

No matter what it is, she clings to him for support.

19 いつもあの人は（   ）しているので、怪しいと思います。

Itsumo ano hito wa (   ) shite iru no de, ayashii to omoimasu.

The way he is always skulking around, I think something strange is going on.

20 若い女性たちが私を見て（   ）笑っているんです。

Wakai josei-tachi ga watashi o mite (   ) waratte iru n' desu.

Looking at me, some young women started snickering.

21 お父さんは、あんな（   ）した男と結婚するなと言ってるわよ。

Otōsan wa, anna (   ) shita otoko to kekkon suru na to itte 'ru wa yo.

Father says you shouldn't marry a flashy guy like that.

22 暑さのせいで、みんな（   ）仕事をしています。

Atsusa no sei de, minna (   ) shigoto o shite imasu.

Because of the heat everyone is working in a kind of stupor.

23 （   ）すると必ず胃が痛くなるんだ。

(   ) suru to kanarazu i ga itaku naru n' da.

When I'm feeling irritated, I invariably get a stomachache.

Answers to the Quizzes

(slashes indicate alternative choices)

A New Lease on Life (pp. 50-53)

1. がんがん (gangan)
2. きりきり (kirikiri)
3. へとへと (hetoheto)
4. きりきり (kirikiri)
5. からから (karakara)
6. からから (karakara)
7. がんがん (gangan)
8. へとへと (hetoheto)
9. どたばた (dotabata)
10. ぺこぺこ (pekopeko)
11. ぺこぺこ (pekopeko)
12. どたばた (dotabata)
13. じたばた (jitabata)
14. すかっと (sukatto)
15. すかっと (sukatto)
16. じたばた (jitabata)
17. ちびちび (chibichibi)
18. ちびちび (chibichibi)
19. どんどん (dondon)
20. ぐうっと／ぐっと (gūtto/gutto)
21. どんどん (dondon)
22. ぐうっと／ぐっと (gūtto/gutto)

A Business Lunch (pp. 70-74)

1. がくんと (gakunto)
2. ぴりぴり (piripiri)
3. ぽちぽち (pochipochi)
4. うかうか (ukauka)
5. きちきち (kichikichi)
6. きちんと (kichinto)
7. ぎりぎり (girigiri)
8. すんなり (sunnari)
9. ずるずる (zuruzuru)
10. すっぱり (suppari)
11. ずばり (zubari)
12. がくんと (gakunto)
13. ぴりぴり (piripiri)
14. ぽちぽち (bochibochi)
15. うかうか (ukauka)
16. ぽちぽち (bochibochi)
17. きちきち (kichikichi)
18. きちんと (kichinto)
19. ぎりぎり (girigiri)
20. すんなり (sunnari)
21. ずるずる (zuruzuru)
22. すっぱり (suppari)
23. ずばり (zubari)

A Man's Place (pp. 86-89)

1. こんがり (kongari)
2. ごろごろ (gorogoro)
3. ぶくぶく (bukubuku)
4. じりじり (jirijiri)
5. こつこつ (kotsukotsu)
6. すらりと (surarito)
7. ずんぐり／ずんぐりむっくり (zunguri/zunguri-mukkuri)
8. がっしり (gasshiri)
9. ぐっすり (gussuri)
10. ぐったり (guttari)
11. こんがり (kongari)
12. ごろごろ (gorogoro)
13. ぶくぶく (bukubuku)
14. じりじり (jirijiri)
15. こつこつ (kotsukotsu)
16. すらりと (surarito)
17. ずんぐり／ずんぐりむっくり (zunguri/zunguri-mukkuri)
18. がっしり (gasshiri)
19. ぐっすり (gussuri)
20. ぐったり (guttari)

A Big Headache (pp. 103-106)

1. むかむか (mukamuka)
2. くらくら (kurakura)
3. くどくど (kudokudo)
4. げんなり (gennari)
5. べろべろ (berobero)
6. ばりばり (baribari)
7. ぐいぐい (guigui)
8. うつらうつら (utsura-utsura)
9. たっぷり (tappuri)
10. うとうと (utouto)
11. うっかり (ukkari)
12. むかむか (mukamuka)
13. くらくら (kurakura)
14. くどくど (kudokudo)
15. げんなり (gennari)
16. べろべろ (berobero)
17. ばりばり (baribari)
18. ぐいぐい (guigui)
19. うとうと／うつらうつら (utouto/utsura-utsura)
20. たっぷり (tappuri)
21. うとうと／うつらうつら (utouto/utsura-utsura)
22. うっかり (ukkari)

Feeling Out of Sorts? (pp. 117-120)

1. ひりひり (hirihiri)
2. ぜいぜい (zeizei)
3. こんこん (konkon)
4. ごほんごほん (gohongohon)

5. ぞくぞく (zokuzoku)
6. ひやひや (hiyahiya)
7. もりもり (morimori)
8. しょぼしょぼ (shoboshobo)
9. しくしく (shikushiku)
10. ひりひり (hirihiri)
11. ぜいぜい (zeizei)

12. こんこん (konkon)
13. ごほんごほん (gohongohon)
14. ぞくぞく (zokuzoku)
15. ひやひや (hiyahiya)
16. もりもり (morimori)
17. しょぼしょぼ (shoboshobo)
18. しくしく (shikushiku)

The Trials of Middle Managers (pp. 132-135)

1. やきもき (yakimoki)
2. やんわり (yanwari)
3. ばしっと (bashitto)
4. ぷうっと (pūtto)
5. ぼけっと (boketto)
6. ぼそぼそ (bosoboso)
7. ぶすっと (busutto)
8. めそめそ (mesomeso)
9. ぎゃあぎゃあ (gyāgyā)
10. やきもき (yakimoki)

11. やんわり (yanwari)
12. ばしっと (bashitto)
13. ぷうっと (pūtto)
14. ぼけっと (boketto)
15. ぼそぼそ (bosoboso)
16. ぐずぐず (guzuguzu)
17. ぐずぐず (guzuguzu)
18. ぶすっと (busutto)
19. めそめそ (mesomeso)
20. ぎゃあぎゃあ (gyāgyā)

A Spat (pp. 147- 150)

1. じいっと／じっと (jītto/jitto)
2. ぷりぷり (puripuri)
3. ぴちぴち (pichipichi)
4. ぞうっと／ぞっと (zōtto/zotto)
5. にたにた (nitanita)
6. いちゃいちゃ (ichaicha)
7. そわそわ (sowasowa)
8. ちやほや (chiyahoya)
9. ぶよぶよ (buyobuyo)
10. めろめろ (meromero)

11. じいっと／じっと (jītto/jitto)
12. ぷりぷり (puripuri)
13. ぴちぴち (pichipichi)
14. ぞうっと／ぞっと (zōtto/zotto)
15. にたにた (nitanita)
16. いちゃいちゃ (ichaicha)
17. そわそわ (sowasowa)
18. ちやほや (chiyahoya)
19. ぶよぶよ (buyobuyo)
20. めろめろ (meromero)

Smoothing Things Over (pp. 163-166)

1. つるつる (tsurutsuru)
2. てかてか (tekateka)
3. せっせと (sesseto)
4. ぴしゃぴしゃ (pishapisha)
5. めきめき (mekimeki)
6. じわじわ (jiwajiwa)
7. ぴたり／ぴったり (pitari/pittari)
8. しっとり (shittori)
9. つやつや (tsuyatsuya)
10. すべすべ／つるつる (subesube/tsurutsuru)
11. つるつる (tsurutsuru)
12. てかてか (tekateka)
13. せっせと (sesseto)
14. ぴしゃぴしゃ (pishapisha)
15. めきめき (mekimeki)
16. じわじわ (jiwajiwa)
17. ぴったり (pittari)
18. しっとり (shittori)
19. つやつや (tsuyatsuya)
20. すべすべ (subesube)

"Pretty Woman" (pp. 179-183)

1. はらはら (harahara)
2. どきどき (dokidoki)
3. ぽうっと (pōtto)
4. ぱっと／ぱあっと (patto/pātto)
5. うっとり (uttori)
6. しっかり (shikkari)
7. しっかり (shikkari)
8. はっきり (hakkiri)
9. うんざり (unzari)
10. がばがば (gabagaba)
11. がばがば (gabagaba)
12. がっくり (gakkuri)
13. はらはら (harahara)
14. どきどき (dokidoki)
15. ぽうっと (pōtto)
16. ぱっと (patto)
17. ぱっと／ぱあっと (patto/pātto)
18. うっとり (uttori)
19. しっかり (shikkari)
20. しっかり (shikkari)
21. はっきり (hakkiri)
22. うんざり (unzari)
23. がばがば (gabagaba)
24. がっくり (gakkuri)

A Romantic Affair (pp. 196-199)

1. ふわっと (fuwatto)
2. さらさら (sarasara)
3. ぺしゃんこ／ぺちゃんこ (peshanko/pechanko)
4. ごわごわ (gowagowa)
5. ぼさぼさ (bosabosa)
6. くっきり (kukkiri)

7. ふんわり／ふわり
   (funwari/fuwari)
8. ぺたんと (petanto)
9. ちりちり (chirichiri)
10. ばっちり (batchiri)
11. ふんわり／ふわり
   (funwari/fuwari)
12. さらさら (sarasara)
13. ぺしゃんこ／ぺちゃんこ
   (peshanko/pechanko)

14. ごわごわ (gowagowa)
15. ぼさぼさ (bosabosa)
16. くっきり (kukkiri)
17. ふんわり／ふわり
   (funwari/fuwari)
18. ぺたんと (petanto)
19. ちりちり (chirichiri)
20. ばっちり (batchiri)

The Rush Hour (pp. 213-216)

1. ぎゅうぎゅう (gyūgyū)
2. だらだら (daradara)
3. くたくた (kutakuta)
4. べとべと／べたべた
   (betobeto/betabeta)
5. べたべた (betabeta)
6. べったり／べたべた／べとべと
   (bettari/betabeta/betobeto)
7. こそこそ (kosokoso)
8. くすくす (kusukusu)
9. ちゃらちゃら (charachara)
10. でれでれ (deredere)
11. いらいら (iraira)
12. ぎゅうぎゅう (gyūgyū)

13. だらだら (daradara)
14. だらだら (daradara)
15. くたくた (kutakuta)
16. べとべと／べたべた
   (betobeto/betabeta)
17. べたべた (betabeta)
18. べったり (bettari)
19. こそこそ (kosokoso)
20. くすくす (kusukusu)
21. ちゃらちゃら (charachara)
22. でれでれ／だらだら
   (deredere/daradara)
23. いらいら (iraira)

BIBLIOGRAPHY

『A Practical Guide to Japanese-English Onomatopoeia & Mimesis 日英擬音・擬態語活用辞典』尾野秀一編著（北星堂書店, 1984）

『現代擬音語擬態語用法辞典』飛田良文・浅田秀子著（東京堂出版, 2002）

『擬音語・擬態語』外国人のための日本語例文・問題シリーズ14　名柄迪監修、日向茂男・日比谷潤子著（荒竹出版, 1989）

『擬音語・擬態語辞典』浅野鶴子・金田一春彦著（角川書店, 1978）

『正しい意味と用法がすぐわかる擬音語・擬態語使い方辞典』阿刀田稔子・星野和子著（創拓社, 1993）

『＜和英＞擬音語・擬態語分類用法辞典』アンドルー・C・チャン著（大修館書店, 1990）

"Dictionary of English Phonesthemes," Benjamin K. Shisler (http://www.geocities.com/SoHo/Studios/9783/phond1.html)

"Linguistic Iconism," Roger W. Westcott (Language: Journal of Linguistic Society of America vol. 47 (2), 1971)

"Ka-BOOM!: A Dictionary of Comicbook Words on Historical Principles," Kevin J. Taylor (http://collection.nlc-bnc.ca/100/200/300/ktaylor/kaboom/Kaboomhome.htm)

"The Sound-Symbolic System of Japanese," Shoko Saito Hamano (doctoral dissertation, University of Florida, 1986)

ONOMATOPOEIA INDEX
(in a, i, u, e, o, order)

GENERAL INDEX

slip 67

slope 206

sloppy 211

slovenly 211

slowly 46, 62

slowly but steadily 159

slowly but surely 82

slurping 67, 155, 156

sly 209

smacking 156

small *tsu* (つ) 24

smash 10, 13

smile 142

smirk 142

smooth 66, 155, 156, 162, 188, 193

snap 11

sneaky 209

snicker 32

sniffing 67

sniffling 115

sniveling 130

snort 32, 126

snuffling 67

soba (そば) 155, 156

sociability 130

soft 124, 157, 160, 188

soggy 146

solid 83, 174

somber 173

somehow 186

sōmen (そうめん) 156

something 186

sonna koto wa nai (そんなことはない) 153

sono sen de (その線で) 57

soothing 160

sore wa nai (それはない) 153

sorry 138

sort of 186

sound 9

sound symbolism 13, 16, 19, 20

sound-imitating 20

soy sauce 207

soybeans 176

spaghetti 155

sparkling 161

spatter 158

spectacular 173

speech 31

speech and action 47

spend 177

spiciness 61

spineless 146

spirited 141

spite 143

splash 10, 158

splat 13

split 61, 125

spoil 145

spreading 173

squawk 12

squeeze 205

squelchy 145

squinty eyes 114

squishy 145

st- 13

stable 13

stalwart 13

standard Japanese 59

stands to reason 77

starchy 191

staring down 97

staunch 13

steadfast 13

steady 13, 46, 62, 82, 98, 157

stick out one's tongue 97

sticky 188, 207, 208

（改訂版）日本語の擬音語・擬態語
Jazz Up Your Japanese with Onomatopoeia

2003 年 7 月　第 1 刷発行
2008 年 5 月　第 4 刷発行

著　者　福田浩子

発行者　富田 充

発行所　講談社インターナショナル株式会社
　　　　〒112-8652　東京都文京区音羽 1-17-14
　　　　電話　03-3944-6493（編集部）
　　　　　　　03-3944-6492（営業部・業務部）
　　　　ホームページ　www.kodansha-intl.com

印刷・製本所　大日本印刷株式会社

落丁本、乱丁本は購入書店名を明記のうえ、講談社インターナショナル業務部宛
にお送りください。送料小社負担にてお取替えいたします。なお、この本について
のお問い合わせは、編集部宛にお願いいたします。本書の無断複写（コピー）
は著作権法上での例外を除き、禁じられています。

定価はカバーに表示してあります。

© 福田浩子 2003
Printed in Japan
ISBN 978-4-7700-2956-0